I Hope You'll Still Love Me:
An LGBTQIA+ South Asian Anthology

Edited by: Nithya Elsa Ramesh

Print ISBN: 978-1-7368513-0-2
E-Book ISBN: 978-1-7368513-1-9

Printed in the United States of America
Edited by Nithya Elsa Ramesh
Cover design by payal kumar
First Edition, 2021

To my parents,

I love you. Thank you.

To everyone that touched this project,

Your help and support in creating this collection was
invaluable.

To every Queer South Asian reading this,

There are more of us than you know and together we will
change the world.

Table of Contents

Introduction

Nithya Elsa Ramesh (she/her)

Someone once said that freedom is nothing but the distance between a bird and its cage. Yet, what do we do when the cage we attempt to escape from is a friend, a parent, a loved one? We yearn for freedom from the expectations they might hold for us, the molds they need us to fit into, or the conditional love they offer us, yet we care for them so dearly that freedom becomes a distant dream. We hide or begrudgingly adjust, hoping they'll still love us.

This sentiment is nowhere more valid than within the South Asian diaspora, i.e., people descending from Afghanistan, Bangladesh, Bhutan, India, Maldives, Nepal, Pakistan, and Sri Lanka. As a community, we relate to the experience of pulling away from the confines of our identity while not wanting to relinquish the beautiful culture and people that shaped us. The added layer of identifying as LGBTQIA+, an umbrella term referring to gender and sexual orientations that deviate from the societal norm of heterosexual and cisgender, complicates our relationship with our South Asian identity. Navigating what it means to be lesbian, gay, bisexual, transgender, intersex, asexual, pansexual, polyamorous, and more, in addition to being South Asian, is complex, frustrating, and wonderful. Unfortunately, it is often an experience ignored in mainstream storytelling.

When I first began compiling this anthology, I felt alone in my intersectional experience of being pansexual and South Asian. I had spent a large part of my twenty-two years concealing my sexuality from my family while stealthily searching bookshelves and the internet for stories that spoke to my queerness. Overwhelmed with coming out stories that ended with tearful acceptances, pats on the back, and the welcoming arms of a queer community that looked just like them, I knew these tales were not my own. They failed to explore the complexities that come from brown-ness and queerness, individually and interwoven: the double-pronged societal rejection that pushes us out of the "norm" of both communities. While the brown community often rejects us for our queerness, we are fetishized or invisibilized in the queer community for being brown.

In June of 2020, trapped within the four walls of my apartment in Ann Arbor, Michigan, 8,890 miles away from my family, and looking for a sense of identity, I decided to gather these stories myself. Through submission rounds and interviews, I heard a similar resounding and affirming notion: we want to create what we did not have growing up.

And here it is.

I Hope You'll Still Love Me speaks to people often swept under the rug and tells them that other South Asians feel, hurt, and love just like they do. The book aspires to touch families and loved ones who struggle to understand the whats, whys, and hows of love and life like this. In writing and compiling this book, the hope is that, beyond answering these questions, it provides insight and creates understanding and acceptance. This collection is not intended to be a political statement, yet, often, when misunderstood groups of people share their personal experiences, they in and of themselves become political. So, maybe this is political. Or perhaps this is the beginning of a conversation that has been disregarded for centuries.

Existing as an LGBTQIA+ person in the South Asian community is not easy. Homophobic barriers are dressed up as "tradition," "culture," "religion," and "reputation," hiding their ugly roots of ancient colonialist thinking. This book follows the personal experiences of numerous South Asian individuals of different religions, ages, nationalities, and genders through a series of personal stories. Each story offers a glimpse into how the intersection of their ethnicity and sexuality influences their lives, families, careers, and relationships.

I spent around a year conducting interviews, collecting stories, and transforming deeply personal tales into the book you now hold in your hands. I am eternally grateful to those who wrote their own stories and worked with me to polish them and those who unfolded their life through interviews and allowed me to put pen to paper for them.

Bringing this book to life was akin to breaking down a reservoir wall of the kind untruths, masks, and buried emotions that people like us use to protect ourselves from the realities of our intersectional identities. This experience forced me to face the gushing river of hurt, rejection, and isolation that plagued my understanding of being LGBTQIA+ and South Asian and somehow find the dancing rays of sunlight when the water ran still.

The contributors who were brave enough to share their secrets with me became this light and taught me how beautiful, powerful, and diverse our experiences truly are. Each story invites you into their world, offering additional insight through contributors' biographies, including their pronouns, passions, and perspectives. The inclusion of gender pronouns was intentional to acknowledge that gender means different things to different people and can not be assumed. Through a peek into their passions and perspectives, readers gain a deeper understanding of how this intersection of identities shaped the people the contributors have become.

On these pages, I found a community of compassionate, vulnerable, and inspiring people that taught me strength in the face of adversity. Through tales of vulnerability, heartbreak, and triumph, contributors lay their truth out for readers. These narratives explore coming out to yourself and family and friends, falling in love, recovering from heartbreak, battling body image issues, searching for spaces to be simultaneously queer and South Asian, the influence of fanfiction, navigating religion, the demand for perfection, transracial adoption, being transgender and South Asian, gender confirmation surgery, finding community, and so much more.

We attempt to bring these abstract concepts to life through each personal account, punctuated by relatable people and experiences. There might be stories you disagree with, and that's okay. This book aims to be authentic towards these personal, mostly lived, experiences.

However, I would also like to acknowledge that there are missing voices. Among others, I recognize an imbalance in gender and sex representation in this collection, specifically regarding masculine, third gender, and intersex perspectives. I realize that many stories highlight a U.S.-centric experience and are not exhaustive of all South Asian ethnicities. This book is far from being the solution we have been searching for. Instead, this is just the beginning.

I do not expect this to be the end of my career advocating for Queer South Asian representation; far from it. For so long as society remains stagnant and silent, people like us must share our stories. The written word will remain the most influential tool we have to battle the tyrant of today and tradition, to remind the world that we exist, we have existed, and we aren't going anywhere.

We hope you will still love us.

part 1:

to those who love me

When Tulips Bloom in Michigan
Trigger warning: mention of suicide
Shaji Mathews

My mother sat on the sofa. I was on the chair across from her. She looked at me expectantly. This was the moment. I couldn't wait any longer. "Amma, I am not going to get married," I said.

She was visiting me from India after a stay in New York with my brother. It was her first visit to my apartment, the one I was finally able to afford to rent by myself. Gone was the roach-infested off-campus student apartment that I shared with two others. I had graduated, found a decent job, and moved to my own place six months ago. She had wanted to visit from the day I signed the lease, but I kept holding back until I was settled. I was also avoiding this inevitable conversation.

I knew I couldn't avoid the topic any longer. While my friends were getting married in India, I was getting ready to go to the USA. Once I landed, my priority was securing an American degree followed by a reputable job. Working part-time and attending school was not the right time to consider getting married and everyone in the family understood.

But now what? Amma broached the topic as soon as I picked her up from the Detroit airport terminal Friday evening. It wasn't an outright demand but a forewarning that we would need to discuss some of the proposals she and the family had been entertaining for me. "Amma, you just landed," I said, biding for time.

It was late in the evening by the time we got to my apartment after stopping for dinner on the way. I had my bed ready for her and took the sofa for myself. She promised to check the pantry first thing in the morning and make a grocery list of items to shop for so that she could prepare a proper meal with all my favorite dishes.

Saturday morning was for sleeping in, if not for my mother's moving around in the kitchen. By the time I woke up, she had made coffee and breakfast with things she could find in the pantry. We went shopping for items she insisted I must have in my apartment. Amma went on a cooking spree once we got home. By 7:00 PM, dinner was on the table. Indeed, all my favorite dishes. Admittedly, I ate like I hadn't eaten in months.

It wasn't until after we put the dishes away, cleaned the kitchen, and sat down that she asked what my plans were for marriage. "If you have someone in mind, please tell me, even if it's an American girl," she added. "If not, you have to let us help you find someone."

"Amma, I am not going to get married," I said.

Amma was surprised. "What's the hurdle now, Son? School is done, you have a good job, what are you waiting for?" She asked.

"Amma, I am gay." I blurted out.

There was no taking it back now. Words I had wanted to articulate to my mother for so many years just fell out of my mouth. I was surprisingly calm.

I had been planning for this moment for so long.

I knew I was attracted to men since my teens, and I have fought it ever since. During my adolescent years in India, there were hardly any resources to help me understand what I was going through. Some of the rare references in books and popular psychology magazines I had access to said homosexual feelings in adolescents could be a passing phase. I truly wanted to believe that was the case with me.

I was considered to be a good boy by all: studious, religious, obedient. I wasn't distracted by chasing after girls, and my community thought that was a good thing. I didn't chase after boys either because the Catholic church taught me that same-sex attraction was a sin if I acted upon it. Plenty of male bonding with friends took care of my emotional needs through my late teens and early twenties. All the while, I was fighting the physical attraction I felt towards some.

Surrounded by lives full of love and romance, I masked my loneliness. My friends were falling in love or getting married and moving on. Every one of them and their new spouses wanted me to find the happiness they had. Denying myself all that happiness was just so painful.

Finally, I summoned the courage to seek help when I was twenty-four. I found the name of a psychiatrist in a Malayalam* magazine's advice column and went to see him without the knowledge of any of my friends or family. I told the doctor I had homosexual feelings and was struggling with it. He responded matter-of-factly, explaining that homosexuality was natural and no longer considered to be a medical condition to be treated. There are a lot of people living openly as homosexuals in countries like America and parts of

Europe, he said. There are homosexuals in India as well, but the conditions for them are still undesirable, he cautioned. While he didn't believe that it was a passing phase for me, his advice was to not act on my feelings until I was ready to face the consequences. Homosexuality was a crime in India, he warned me.

Maybe I could continue hiding as long as I didn't act on my urges. But the feeling of isolation and self-loathing had gotten worse.

I kept wondering if there was a cure for my condition that the psychiatrist didn't know of. Perhaps it was a passing phase after all, and drugs or therapy could change me.

A few months later, I searched for and found another psychiatrist in a different city. This one didn't take long to jump right on to a fix for me.

"Have you had sex yet?" he asked. I was in my mid-twenties. I had no sexual experience, gay or straight, at that point. I said no.

"How do you know what you want without even trying?" he asked. "Go home, get married, it will work out. If not, come again. I will treat you." That was how he dismissed me.

I was furious. I didn't want my future to be an experiment. If it failed, I would be a lifetime patient for him or other therapists.

So, after a few months, when the opportunity to migrate to America arose, I took it. When I left the shore of India, I hoped and prayed that a different environment would somehow change me to a heterosexual.

Neither the water nor the air in America magically transformed my sexual orientation, and it did not take long to confirm my sexual identity. Reaching that conclusion was one thing; understanding, accepting and celebrating it was the hard part. How was I going to face my family? How would they receive this new me? I would rather die than face the consequences of coming out, I thought.

Somehow, the thought of killing myself fizzled once I got busy with graduate school and friends and occasional sexual encounters. There were days when I would get so depressed about the future that it felt like I couldn't go on. Then, I would meet someone I thought I could fall in love with, and hope would spring forth. Slowly, I started accepting myself as a gay male even though I had not come out to anyone. Physical distance from my family helped. It was easy to pretend to have a different life on the phone and not face to face.

But, graduation and job interviews, and employment followed. Once I settled into my own apartment, my mother wanted to visit. And I knew I had to come out of this dark closet to her before I did so with anyone else. She had been the most supportive in all my endeavors, be it art, studies, or writing. For someone from her generation, she demonstrated an open mind about many things. If she could understand and accept me, I didn't care if the rest of the family did or did not.

And there she was, in my apartment living room, asking me why I wouldn't get married. All the logically ordered answers I had prepared in my head just vanished.

She kept looking at me like she didn't hear me the first time I said I was gay.

"I am gay," I repeated with a quiver in my voice. I didn't want to use the Malayalam word for homosexual, which put the focus on the "sex" part rather than me as a whole person.

Amma looked at me in shock.

"What are you saying, my son?" she asked after a moment of silence.

"Amma, I am attracted to men, not women. I can't get married to a woman."

"But you are so well balanced and nothing like those gays on TV. How could you be gay? Can't you change? There must be a cure for this. This is America after all." Amma at least knew the word "gay" from TV.

"Amma, this is who I am. I was born this way, and I can't change it. And I don't want to pretend that I am something I am not." I tried to explain.

"But when you left India, you were not like this. It must be the diet here that turned you this way. I wish you never left India. This kind of thing is never heard of in India." Amma went on.

"Amma, I was like this in India and will be like this no matter where I live. It just took this long for me to accept myself for who I am." I said.

"But what about having a family? How about children? Who will take care of you when you get older? How will you face society?" It was a barrage of questions.

"Amma, I will deal with all that. I don't want to bring a woman into my life knowing full well that I can't give her the life she deserves. How would you feel if one of my sisters got married to someone gay?" I offered.

Amma went quiet.

"There must have been something wrong the way we brought you up." She said.

"Amma, there was nothing wrong with the way you brought me up. Knowing that I have a loving mother gave me strength all these years to deal with this."

I was choking up. Tears were running down Amma's cheeks. She lifted the end of her *sari* and wiped them away. I knew there was so much more to explain, but I couldn't wait any longer. I moved towards her and hugged her.

She hugged me back and whispered in my ears the words I had been waiting to hear for so many years.

"Whatever it is, you are still my son, and my love for you won't change."

We stayed on the sofa, hugging each other for a long time before eventually going to bed.

The following day, we went to the tulip festival on the state's west side. It was a clear sunny spring day in Michigan, and I was giddy with joy. During the two-hour drive, she continued asking me questions, but I was better prepared emotionally to answer them this time. I explained how natural homosexuality felt to me, just as heterosexuality did for most people. And how diverse humankind is in terms of gender, color, and sexual identity. And how dull the universe would be if it were monochromatic.

Tulips and daffodils were blooming all over the town inside and outside the festival venue. We were wandering by a large bed of yellow tulips with a few stray bright orange flowers. Amma stopped and bent over to look closely at one of the orange flowers. She looked up at me with a sparkle in her eyes.

I knew what she meant.

Contributor's Bio:

Shaji Mathews (he/him) is a gay male born and brought up in Kerala, India. Until his mid-twenties, he brushed his gayness aside as a passing phase. Being brought up in a Catholic family left him with a lot of guilt to deal with. When he decided between marrying a woman under societal pressure and continuing to live in India or moving to the USA under the pretense of a better career, he chose the latter. He finally accepts himself as who he is, has come out to his family and friends, and has found love. He has reached out to other South Asian LGBTQIA+ folks over the years and co-founded Trikone Michigan in 1996. His immigrant angst paired with the internalized homophobia, classism, and racism he fights every day within himself led to this story's creation.

To my Mother, on Queerness, Women of Color, and Revolutionary Love

Maya Bhardwaj

I never truly came out to my mother. She and my father's approach to my previous partner were largely a Don't Ask Don't Tell approach: if they didn't ask, I wouldn't tell. He was a formerly incarcerated Jamaican-American man and an activist I met through criminal justice organizing in South Florida. They disapproved of him, were dismayed that he hadn't been to college, and felt he wasn't a good fit: hence, in our conversations, we pretended he didn't exist. There was little space to discuss that he and I were in a non-monogamous relationship and were experimenting with polyamory - or that I was embracing my pansexuality and was exploring relationships with women and nonbinary people as well.

My relationship with him, stressed by financial precarity, harassment by the police, and exhaustion brought on by activism, turned abusive when we moved to Costa Rica for his work after four years together. I left him, feeling broken, and spent six months wandering around Central America. I learned from indigenous and socialist guerrilleros, climbed volcanoes, and marveled at the sea. Months later, I pieced myself together enough to return to organizing and the US. I told my parents nothing of why my ex and I broke up: I was unwilling to confirm their suspicions with a racist trope.

After leaving Central America, I moved to New York to work as a housing organizer. At first, I casually dated several leftist men of color activists and artists who mirrored my ex. Their traumas and triggers, combined with mine, resulted in rollercoaster relationships that didn't last. After these fractured and frustrating experiences, I vowed I was done with men. I wanted a relationship that was sweeter, softer, more open. I wanted something that felt like home and not like a struggle when I returned.

I was inspired by the brilliant femmes I met organizing for a better world, and I wanted a movement partner with whom I could reignite my belief in revolutionary love.

My mother and I have always been extremely close. Even when I lied to her face as a rebellious teenager, there were few secrets she didn't see through. She nurtured my art and music and spooled out my questions, encouraging my insatiable curiosity. She put me in a leftist "hippie school" when I was five. A school that molded us into little activists inspired by the founders' experience with student uprisings in the 1960s. We studied feminist readings of the Odyssey and learned from Grace Lee Boggs and Black labor activists, artists, and farmers who were conjuring up an Afrofuturist Detroit. My mother started my violin studies and enrolled me in horseback riding lessons when I was four, proudly bringing the lone Brown girl into the stables.

My mother's father and grandfather were freedom fighters against the Raj, taking arrest for civil disobedience and leading rallies for Indian independence. Her great-grandfather changed his last name from our very caste-privileged "Gothra," choosing to adopt "Rao" as a surname they thought could better communicate their anti-casteist politics. Her mother and aunt were the first women to ride bicycles in Hyderabad. Her mother cycled in *saris* to the university where she worked as a professor, defiantly flouting the gender norms of the day for women of her community. An avowed feminist, she and her sisters gave me the Communist Manifesto to read when I was ten years old.

My mother is the reason I came to organizing, and she always supported – and shared – my fierce identity as an anti-capitalist, feminist, woman of color. Those pieces of my identity were never the issue. But queerness was something else.

I think my mother always knew that I was queer at some level. My heartbreaks over slights from childhood female friends were over the top even for the emotional, very Pisces, artsy and musical kid I was from a young age. I frequently drew portraits of my female classmates in my sketchbook, serenaded my female friends with my violin, and mooned over lady knights and sorceresses in the fantasy books I voraciously devoured. I was constantly crushing on the few older South Asian girls in my class, especially the cool, slim, tall, young women who flitted effortlessly in and out of white spaces. These were girls who I both yearned to be like and yearned for, though I was too short, dark-skinned, hairy, and awkward to be like them or to be an object of their desire.

So I chose not to come out to my mother formally but to tell her in the way that felt most natural to me. We were on the phone for our weekly check-ins as I sat in a park on the waterfront in Harlem and fiddled with my bike. She asked me how I was spending my free time in New York, and I told her that I had been dating a bit. She asked me to describe the people I liked. "There's a few guys I've been talking to who are interesting, and there's this woman I've been on a couple of dates with...I'm not sure where it's going, but she's brilliant and really sweet."

My mother paused briefly but hardly missed a beat. "A woman?" she repeated.

"Yes," I responded, silently challenging her to say something further.

But she surprised me with her response. "It's good you're dating women," she said. "Maybe then you won't end up some man's servant. Men are useless - especially Indian men - they just want someone to replace their mother. You won't have to cook and clean for a slob who ruins your life while working full-time like me."

I laughed, incredulous. "Thanks for the life advice, Mum," I said. "You're welcome," she told me, laughing back. And like that, we moved on to talking about my work and our latest housing justice campaign.

For my mother's 60th birthday, my girlfriend at the time and I came home in secret to surprise her. It was the first time they met in person. My parents had heard about her and were pleased that she was a Ph.D. student and an adjunct professor. They liked that she was studying environmental racism in her hometown in Upstate New York, researching the toxic waste processing plants that had likely triggered her mother's inexplicable mouth cancer. For them, she was respectable, stable: a "good head on her shoulders," in their words. She fit their ideals shaped by casteism and classism so it didn't matter to them that she was Black.

My mom cooked *saru*, a South Indian tomato lentil soup, and *menaskai*, a Karnataka style curry, for my girlfriend and watched approvingly as she asked for seconds. My girlfriend came with me to the surprise party I had organized for my mom's birthday. She met my mother's close friends, all leftist women who had similarly enrolled their children in my hippie school, and they showered her with encouraging questions and praise. We drove around summertime Detroit and took in the river air. We went to the Allied Media Conference and met my activist comrades from across the country. We hung out with my best friends from childhood, and everyone loved her. For once, things felt simple, calm.

But on our last night in town, we got into a familiar fight. We had been struggling over the disconnects in our dreams for our futures, my wanderlust chafing against her quest for stability, my desire to move us back home to India to raise children who felt like they fit somewhere, incompatible with her mandate to stay close to her family. We shouted at each other, launching barbs in my childhood room. Like the fights before, it ended in her pronouncing our lack of compatibility. I fled downstairs to where my parents were sitting, and my mother silently followed me with her eyes as I aimlessly walked around the house.

"Are you sure this is what you want, Maya?" she asked me finally. "Are you sure you're not confused? This isn't just a phase?"

She watched me as I locked myself in the bathroom, tears streaming down my face. When I emerged, she hugged me, no words exchanged.

A few weeks later, my girlfriend and I went upstate to visit her family for her baby niece's ceremony. Our unresolved fight hung heavy in the air between us, but her family ensconced me with love. I had already met her mother and sisters, and they embraced me warmly as we arrived, all boisterous laughs and loud jokes, with the smell of bacon and collard greens on the stove. We dressed up for church together and held hands in the pews as we sang spirituals in harmony. I gave her sister a children's book about a young Harriet Tubman, and I held the baby, crooning my mother's lullabies in Kannada* to her tiny scrunched-up face.

Faith was a core part of my girlfriend's mother's life. Curious about my own, she had asked me questions about Hinduism when I had visited last. Hoping to provide answers I didn't have, I brought her a book of Tagore's poetry this time, and she flipped through its pages, rapt. Family members came in and out of the house, visiting my girlfriend and greeting the baby, telling stories of success and woe. I mentally compared the noise and laughter in their house, all the generations of their family singing and yelling together since they came north from Alabama, with the quiet at my parents' home, two people alone in silence.

I wondered what it would have been like if my parents and I had stayed in Bangalore with our family. I wondered about my life if we moved back. Would I have all this life, these cousins and uncles, this joy and strife all around me? Could I find this rootedness in India, for myself, for the family that my girlfriend and I were hoping to create? Or would home always be split in two?

I didn't know how to make it all fit.

My girlfriend and I held hands on the bus back to New York together, but the air between us felt cold, laden with uncertainty and the sense of turning away from each other with each touch. At her house, we spoke little and went to sleep, together, but spooning in silence. It tasted like an ending, heavy and bittersweet.

After three and a half years together, and after I had left New York to move to London for school, my girlfriend and I decided to end our romantic relationship and explore being platonic friends. "I'll always love you," she told me. "And I know you'll always love me. But I don't know if you actually like me. I can't be together like this." Our last conversation as a couple was a stuttering Facetime call, her side a sunny winter day in Brooklyn and mine a typical cold and wet London evening.

"I love you," I told her, crying.

"I love you too," she replied. "It's not enough."

I called my mother later that evening, voice quavery and thick with tears. "We broke up," I told her. Then, I added, joking about marriage through my labored breaths, "Want to arrange me?"

"I'm sorry, Maya," she replied. "Are you serious? Man or woman?"

"Either....or neither, non-binary people too," I joked shakily. "You have twice the options." She paused, considering, and then replied thoughtfully. "I don't think I can, Maya," she told me. "I know you want someone political, leftist....I don't know any suitable people like that here. I think you're a bit too weird."

"Thanks to you," I snorted, half-laugh half-cry. We stayed together over the phone in silence, her breaths matching my tears.

"We always liked her, Maya," my mother finally said. "I hope you can stay in touch. Maybe she wasn't good for you, but she was a good person, smart and kind. I hope you find another woman - or man - like her someday."

Contributor's Bio:

Maya Bhardwaj (she/her and they/them) is a community organizer, trainer, facilitator, writer, researcher, artist, and musician who has spent the past ten years building grassroots power of people of color. They spend most of their time on anti-capitalist racial, economic, and gender justice campaigns and organizing work. She plays her violin in Carnatic, bluegrass, jazz, Irish folk, and western classical formations. She also sings on the side. She is a visual artist and art-build facilitator for direct actions and campaigns. They are a proud Dravidian, made in the Detroit area with roots and/or community in Bangalore, Bombay, New York, and Mexico City. They are currently based in London, where they are working on a dissertation at SOAS (University of London) called "Queering Solidarity: South Asian Racialization and Politicization in Solidarity with Black Liberation in the US and the UK." She organizes with several queer people of color formations in London and across the US and supports the work of Haiyya: Organise for Action in India as a board member.

Table 4
Nandini Roy

Dear Mom,

I took Dad out to lunch at the end of twelfth grade. We were sitting at an Italian restaurant about 15 minutes away from home. It was boisterous and busy, and I hoped that would distract the other patrons from what might erupt at Table 4 in the next few minutes. We got our water, ordered a salad for the table, and Dad joked about me paying for the lunch despite having a little over $6 in my bank account. I laughed because Dad laughed. In truth, I could barely register what he said. My hands were sweaty and shaky, and I could feel blood rushing to my head.

In South Asian culture, it's essential to maintain the perception of being a perfect child. This meant: straight A+'s, never getting caught doing something you shouldn't be doing by family or gossiping aunties, getting into a highly acclaimed university, maintaining a respectfully close relationship with your parents, and taking care of your appearances.

I always tried to check all of these boxes. Growing up, I did so because you and Dad told me to and because I witnessed your relationship with *Bhai*, my elder brother, falter when he failed to do so. Then, as I came to terms with my sexuality, I realized that I used "checking these boxes" as a way to overcompensate for what I knew you would believe to be a flaw. I overworked myself into hyper-productivity to subconsciously win your trust and conditional love. I thought maybe if that was the one thing I did wrong, it would be forgivable. Well, Mom, is it?

I thought about coming out to you and Dad in tenth grade when I came out to my entire friend group in our high school cafeteria. I remember the hundreds of questions they asked me, including my type and if any of them fell within this type. The questions were funny at the time but manifested into friends' boyfriends not letting me sleepover at their girlfriends' apartments. I wondered if your acceptance would also come with limitations.

I feel like my entire life has been a revolt against everything you believe in while simultaneously vying for your affirmation and approval. Your disdain for pro-choice sentiments heavily influenced my passion for social justice. But, I won public speaking competitions, graduated from high school with high distinction, and showed off my homemade mutton biryani to all your friends because I knew I needed to earn your respect first. I needed to build myself up to be someone that you were so proud of that you couldn't deny me love. However, the more photos you posted on *Facebook* of how proud I made you, the more I was terrified of that pride being taken away.

And, that brings us back to Table 4.

The waiter had just presented our salad and told us he would be back in a few to get our entrée order. Dad started serving himself and asked if I wanted any. I nodded at him, staring blankly at my plate. He dropped a dollop of creamy salad dressing on my plate and gave me a wink as if saying, *"Kya hua meri jaan? Sab thik ho jayegi. Main hoon na."* ("What's wrong my dear? Everything will be okay. I'm here.")

I don't know if it was intentional, but the wink gave me the slight boost of courage I needed to unravel the knots in my stomach.

"I have kissed boys. And I have dated girls."

The first part wasn't necessary, but it almost felt like this was my opportunity to get all my shortcomings out of the way. Almost like the first would soften the second.

The waiter came back, and before he could begin reading the specials, I burst into tears. Dad turned to the waiter and asked for a few minutes, in that Bond-like tone he puts on when he needs to feign confidence in a moment of confusion.

He asked me why I was crying and if I had expected this to go badly. I nodded, unsure if he was kind because I was clearly a mess or because he registered and accepted everything I just shared with him.

He asked why I never felt comfortable sharing this with him earlier. I couldn't say anything without my voice breaking, so he said, "It's okay, baby, nevermind." And we didn't talk about it for the rest of the lunch.

We got into the car to head home, and out of nowhere, he said, "I've heard it's hard for bisexuals to be satisfied in relationships. Be careful of that." I didn't know how to respond. I had heard that stereotype before but ignored it for the most part. This was the first time I was ever directly confronted with it and asked to address it. Later, he said, "Maybe this is just a phase. Don't tell your mom just yet. You know how she is."

So, I kept this from you.

In retrospect, I don't think he meant any ill will. I think he was genuinely just confused and unsure how to support me. I think he was trying to protect me and protect our relationship. He didn't want something like this to ruin our already strained relationship. Can you blame him?

I remember pushing the limits a few times to see how you would react. Sometimes, I would intentionally slip up while telling a story and say, "girlfriend." The look that crossed your face, like you just bit into a lemon and the sourness tickled your nose, showed me that you were not ready. When I told you that I was spending the weekend with a friend and his boyfriend, you said you weren't comfortable because "I should stay away from people like that." On family calls, Dad would ask me if I had any boyfriends or girlfriends yet, and you would shush him with a "yuck, how could you ask that?" When we watched movies or shows that included LGBTQIA+ storylines, you would screech and groan. Unbeknownst to you, you were telling me everything I needed to know about your thoughts and feelings about me and my choices.

I remember calling Dad after a girl I was talking to took her life at the end of my first year of college. I wasn't sure if he ever told you. I got a tattoo for her on a hidden spot because I knew you would disapprove. When you mistakenly saw it on our family vacation, the shock and disgust on your face told me that you didn't know. So when you asked me what it was for, I couldn't gather the courage to explain.

I wonder how different things could have been if you asked me more about my experience. If you were open-minded and genuinely curious about how I feel and what makes me happy. I wish you took the time to learn what sexuality is and the issues LGBTQIA+ youth face. I wish you would read the articles I sent you and were willing to have honest and vulnerable conversations about what you didn't know and the questions you had. Maybe I could have been more patient in initiating open conversation. But, perhaps you could have made the space between us comfortable enough for me to be me.

Maybe if you had, you would have been at the table with us. But, at the time, I knew in my heart that you weren't ready.

With so much love,
Nandini

Contributor's Bio:

Nandini Roy (she/her) is a recent college graduate with a passion for social justice. Her interests include traveling, reading, and cooking. Nandini has written and performed many pieces about the experiences of being a woman of color during her college career. As of recently, she has been exploring her intersecting identities of being South Asian and LGBTQIA+. This is the first piece she has written about the topic, and she hopes it resonates with many young adults on the brink of coming out to their families.

Dysphoria, Dissonance, and Declaration

Icowyn Nazaawl

as told to Editor

In the sixth grade, I dreamt that I was strutting around a mall in a pair of ripped black jeans, a white v-neck, and a leather jacket. I carried an air of arrogance and cockiness like I had the suave to get anyone I wanted. I held my head high, maintained social ease I could never quite grasp before ... oh yeah, and my soft facial structure and feminine curves were replaced by a sharp jawline and a masculine body.

I remember joking around with some friends in this dream when a girl walked past us. She had long black hair, wore a black leather mini skirt, and smelled like lavender. The moment I saw her, I knew I wanted her to be mine. I walked over to her, and she leaned back onto the wall behind her. I placed my hand on the wall next to her, like a cliche early 2000's rom-com bad boy, and bent over slightly to whisper something in her ear. She giggled nervously, tucking a piece of loose hair behind her ear, and I could feel my confidence rising.

I woke up the next morning, confused yet satisfied, wondering if I *might* be attracted to women. The confidence and joy I got from having a man's body were packed away and forgotten. I spent my middle school and high school years becoming obsessed with diving into my sexuality. I explored bisexuality, pansexuality, and asexuality before settling on the term queer. I think this exploration came as a result of the fact that, at the time, it was easier to navigate sexuality than it was to come to terms with my gender identity. Gender identity wasn't as commonly discussed when I was in middle school, and it was challenging to find someone who could relate to what I was going through.

Then, in college, I met a trans man. They later identified as gender fluid and currently use *she*, *he*, and *they* pronouns. Their story felt overwhelmingly comforting and spoke to the part of me that felt liberated as a man. The trans man told me all about his experiences not fitting in with how other people perceived them and the battle she faced with the femininity that their friends and family forced on them. That night, his story played over and over in my mind, enveloping me like a warm blanket.

I no longer felt alone. It didn't seem strange anymore that while my femininity was reinforced and encouraged by those around me, I secretly craved compliments based on my masculine attributes. I began to lean into my masculinity, whether that was how I dressed or how I held my arms or hands when I spoke. I reveled in getting sick, just to hear my raspy, bassy voice. But, the masculine body language, voice, and gender expression always felt forced and incorrect for my body type.

While I could use my discretion, and a sports bra, to make my chest evident or not, I couldn't say the same about my hips. Since elementary school, peers have nicknamed me "birthing hips" because my hips were so distinctly wide. They would often joke that they could look at my hips across the room and know it was me. There is no gender-affirming surgery for this. Trust me. I looked into it. Over time, this pressure of how others might perceive my gender began to build inside me and erupted into self-invalidation of my gender identity.

I knew that I didn't want to identify as a female anymore, but I still didn't feel comfortable identifying as a trans man. The weight of that title felt scary and overwhelming. I began identifying as genderqueer. This meant that my gender identity does not fall within the binary. I was comfortable using she/her and they/them pronouns, but feminine nouns, like being called "girl" or "lady," made me shudder. This middle ground felt simpler because I didn't feel the need to present a certain way. There was no structure or expectations of what being genderqueer looked like, and I never felt like I wasn't meeting the mark.

While I don't know if people respected it or even understood it, they generally accepted my newly discovered identity as something I wanted and needed. The challenging part was continuously correcting people who addressed me as "ma'am" or other feminine nouns. This was especially difficult because this misgendering predominantly happened with people who know I do not identify as a woman. Since I present femininely, they automatically think 'girl.'

I knew my gender expression would make it harder for people to accept me as a trans man, and this fear made it harder for me to identify as one. It wasn't until my second year in pharmacy school, during a dentistry seminar, that I heard someone speak about their transition process and realized these complexities and incongruencies are not unique to me.

It was during a seminar entitled, "How to Treat a Trans Patient," but the story ended up being more focused on a trans woman's journey growing up as a masculine model, being in the army as a pilot, and embracing her masculinity knowing that she was an attractive man. It wasn't until much later, around her 50's, that she realized she had been suppressing her femininity because she thought she could live with this lie forever. Until one day, she reached what she described as her "why point." Why is she sacrificing her happiness? Why is she letting others dictate what she does with her body? Why do others' opinions matter? She made a point to recognize that she had the privilege of status and a successful career when she decided to embrace her true self. She also made it clear that it was the best decision she had ever made.

Her story summarized all the reasons I had been avoiding identifying as trans. She helped me realize that I don't need to "pass" or be on hormone therapy to be a trans man. The gender dysphoria I experienced for so long made me feel like a coward, but now it felt validated. I needed to tell someone how I felt, and, for the first time, it didn't matter how they responded. I just needed to say it out loud because I worried that I likely would've gone back into my "genderqueer" shell if I didn't. I needed to hold on to this revelation and lean into the enlightenment, or its vital purpose might be lost.

I said it out loud to myself, and I said it through tears to a friend. With each declaration, I felt happier and lighter.

But a heaviness set in when I had to return to the heteronormative and sometimes transphobic pharmacy school curriculum. After my school eliminated the brief lecture on hormone replacement therapy, students and professors didn't have any guidance to think outside of the binary. I made all of this progress in expanding my definition of my own gender identity, just for my peers and professors to restrict their thinking.

During my first year, we had a virtual pharmacy activity where we were given an image of a patient and had to come up with questions we would ask them to understand what medication to prescribe to them. Points were taken off if you asked someone that was male presenting if they were pregnant, ignoring the fact that you never know what kind of genitalia someone has. I sat through women's health classes where professors corresponded having a vagina with being a girl. I endured lectures that disregarded trans patients by explaining that ovarian cancer only affects women.

This close-mindedness made me fear how people might respond to my trans identity, so I never came out as a trans man to a single person while in pharmacy school. Instead, I channeled my horror into speaking out against this transphobia to my peers. But they were never as upset or outraged as I was, and my efforts were typically met with their defense of the status quo. This frustrated me even more, but I never stopped trying to challenge the norm.

To silence me, professors and peers often recommended I be careful of deterring conservative patients from wanting to build relationships with me. In response, I brought up the possibility of treating trans patients; I was ignored.

I also challenged the pronouns doctors would put into medical records for trans patients during my clinical and experiential classes. Doctors would note the patient's gender at the top but change pronouns back and forth throughout the report. Besides being confusing to the medical professionals relying on the notes to make decisions, it felt disrespectful to patients. It made me question how we could provide adequate care to them.

To be fair, I understand how challenging it can be to use the correct pronouns. In fact, I still struggle with it. It's tough unlearning a life of societal values and norms. But, I also know how frustrating it is to be frequently misgendered and to constantly explain my gender identity and my dislike for feminine nouns, and sometimes feminine pronouns, to people just for them to forget or make a big deal about it.

Some of the best responses I have received when I tell someone how I identify is when they are casual about it. Something along the lines of, "Okay, cool, thank you for sharing. I appreciate you letting me know because it has probably been sitting with you for a while." Then, swiftly changing the way they address me. Many friends have made the conscious decision of becoming more aware of the trans community and the issues we face since I have shared my identity with them, and that growth has been beautiful. This made me wonder how my classmates and professors might have responded if I did come out during pharmacy school. Would this have pushed them to consider science and medicine outside of the binary? Might it have encouraged others to come out? Could I have found a community that looked like me within the medical field?

Part of what made coming to terms with my trans identity so tough was feeling alone. I felt alone in confronting peers and professors, I felt alone in my trans identity, and I felt alone in my trans South Asian identity. Not only was it challenging for me to find trans representation in the healthcare industry, but I also battled with the lack of Trans-South Asian representation in general. As a South Asian American, I found it hard to identify with the third gender community in India because the challenges they face are so uniquely different from my own. While they identify as neither male nor female. On the other hand, I identify as a trans male, and there is no documentation of this identity that I could find in South Asian literature or history. This left me with white European terminology – and amidst the English and Latin vocabulary, something felt amiss.

It wasn't until a few years ago that I found a Queer South Asian organization based in Chicago. I reached out to them and attended one of their bimonthly Bollywood Drag Show/Dance Party events. Drag queens donned a beautiful full face of makeup, a decadent *sari*, and some opted to keep their facial hair. It felt cathartic to watch them play with gender expression in this way. While there was still a lack of representation of drag kings, being at this event made me more confident about my gender identity. This space empowered the duality of my queerness and brownness.

It is a slowly progressing journey, battling my dissonance between gender expression and gender identity. I have worked hard to understand that gender is a flexible concept and that your gender identity doesn't always have to match your gender expression. At the end of the day, none of it matters, as long as you are comfortable with how you identify as a person. If you choose to change your mind at some point, you have the agency to make it whatever you want. I thrive in the moments a stranger online affirms my gender identity without batting an eye, and I am still learning how to pick my battles with those close to me. I still visibly flinch when my parents call me their "daughter" or when strangers hold doors open for me, saying "ladies first."

There is no contentment in this journey because there will always be highs and lows. I just hope people who are still learning about this community treat it as an identity they don't know well. I hope they listen to understand and offer empathy without any preconceived notions. And I hope we continue to challenge how gender is understood and practiced in health care, the South Asian community, and beyond, so people like me might not need to face the battles I have.

Contributor's Bio:

Icowyn Nazaawl (he/him) is a recent Doctorate of Pharmacy graduate who is passionate about psychiatric medicine, education, and social justice through policy changes. He loves to travel, play sports (abysmally), and write. Icowyn has been advocating for healthcare changes through small legislative victories and hopes to spend more time advocating for domestic violence survivors. He has recently come to terms with his gender as a trans man and has intersecting identities as queer and Indian American. He hopes to bring these identities and the specific concerns these communities face to light in his practice to ensure they are being treated safely and effectively with empathy.

Ek Ladki Ko Dekha Toh Aisa Laga
I Saw a Girl and Felt Like This

Keerthana
as told to Editor

"That means you're still attracted to boys, right?"

I didn't know how to answer. Obviously, the truth is, yes, I am still attracted to boys. But, agreeing felt like invalidating my identity. It felt like pretending nothing had changed. The way my mother asked this question made it feel like she didn't care that I had just come out to her. In the back of her mind, she saw me with *mehndi* painted hands, adorned in a white *sari* and showered in gold, standing next to a *boy* at the *mandap* (wedding altar). And it hurt.

On the balmy Sunday we had this conversation, we sat in her charcoal Honda CRV, parked outside of the Costco down the street from our house. Mom asked me to go grocery shopping with her and, with just the two of us in the car, I thought this was the perfect opportunity to have *the talk.*

Typically, I hit shuffle on my favorite Tollywood playlist once I settle in the front seat, but my phone stayed in my pocket this time. I felt too frozen to pull it out. Mom didn't say anything but hummed quietly to herself as she drove. I could tell she knew something was up. I wiped my sweaty palms on my mid-wash denim jeans, and I could feel my heart beating like a drum.

Once the quiet became too overwhelming to bear, I worked up the courage to ask her, "what would you do if I wasn't straight?"

Subtle, I know. At the time, I thought I was pretty sly. You know, just asking a genuine question. But, looking back, could I have been more obvious?

She didn't answer for a while. Then, when we eventually pulled into the bustling parking lot, she pushed the gear into park and looked over at me. She seemed concerned. "What do you want to tell me? It's obvious you're holding something in."

My parents and I are best friends. I tell them everything. So, when I came to terms with my bisexuality during my first year at college, my first thought was how to explain this to them. I wasn't sure how to explain it or what they would say, but I expected them to be open-minded. My parents didn't raise my brother and me with a wooden spoon. They didn't enforce a harsh curfew or berate me about my report card, and they never policed my closet. Over everything, they prioritized my health and happiness. They were supportive and loving and everything I could have asked for.

This was partly because my dad didn't have a solid home growing up. He was neglected by an abusive father and spent his formative years jumping from hostels to friends' couches. He made it a point to be the dad he didn't have by giving my brother and me everything we needed to be happy. Growing up, the most common phrase you would hear around my house was, "I'll love you no matter what." And he meant it. I was confident my dad wouldn't have an issue with my sexuality because I have witnessed his empathy and willingness to learn.

His open-mindedness is dumbfounding to me sometimes and is something I aspire to. I've watched him stand barefoot and cold outside of our community temple at the annual Ugadi festival, patiently engaging in respectful conversations with uncles and aunties about topics he completely disagrees with them on. I watch his reflection in the rearview mirror in the car ride home. His eyebrows furrow, and his eyes wander as he ponders over the perspectives they offered him. Over breakfast the next day, he shares that he has completely changed his beliefs about the topic because what the other person shared made sense to him. This might not sound like much, but in South Asian culture, it's a big deal. His love, reassurance, and receptiveness gave me comfort in the fact that he would accept me.

On the other hand, my mother was more silent in her support for my brother and me. Her heart was full of love for us, but she struggled with expressing affection. She grew up in a structured, closed-off home. No one fell outside of the norm, and they all met, if not exceeded, expectations for the "perfect" Indian household. Her family was highly regarded and highly judged within her community. This made her hesitant to new ideas. Still, I always felt like I could open up to her about anything because she maintained an open mind and made it clear to us that there was absolutely nothing more important to her than her family's well-being.

The one challenge in our relationship is something I am almost certain is infused into the DNA of South Asian moms everywhere: her concern for our reputation within our community, i.e., *"janaalu em antaaru?"* ("what will people say?"). Although I tried my best to understand her, especially knowing the scrutiny she was under growing up, it has always been a point of contention between us. I was nervous about what she would think this new identity meant for how our family will be perceived. Additionally, over the years, I heard her occasionally say things about the LGBTQIA+ community that convinced me she wouldn't be as understanding.

Once, we were driving home from elementary school, and our neighbor and his husband were outside watering their lawn. They waved to us, and my mom waved back. Then, she turned to me and said, "You know, they're G-A-Y." She spelled it out like it was a curse word and had a look of shock spread across her face. It seems small, but when I came to terms with my sexuality years later, that memory played on loop in my mind.

Now, it was winter break of my freshman year, and I was home for the holidays. I wasn't as talkative, and my parents could tell my mood was different. My entire first semester of college was challenging, to be honest. I was diagnosed with depression my senior year of high school, and being away from home and my support system for four straight months was challenging. I was homesick, I missed my friends, and now this. Although my parents were as supportive as ever, I immediately thought of worst-case scenarios: What if they kick me out? What if I can't afford to finish school? What if I just hold this in forever?

Then, one evening while mindlessly scrolling through YouTube, the trailer for "Ek Ladki Ko Dekha Toh Aisa Laga" came on. The movie stars Sonam Kapoor and follows her journey coming to terms with her queer sexuality while facing pressure to marry a man. Before I realized it, tears were streaming down my face. I collapsed on my bed and felt my chest tighten, and my breath get heavier. I held my hand over my mouth to trap the noise so that my parents couldn't hear me from the next room. I hadn't watched the movie yet, and I had no idea if it was any good, but seeing a South Asian character in a mainstream Bollywood film coming out to her family watered the flower in me that had been aching to bloom. I knew I needed to tell them.

But now, stewing in the silence in that car, I was questioning myself. Would living my truth be worth changing my relationship with my parents forever? Would I even have a relationship with my parents after this? I knew that if I didn't say anything, I would suffocate. And I didn't know if my mental health could recover if I held it in any longer.

"I'm bisexual."

I started crying and turned towards my window, away from her. I hid my face in my shoulder, hoping she couldn't see me. I felt embarrassed. I don't know why.

Worst-case scenarios flashed through my mind again: What if Mom never talks to me again? What if my parents don't let me hang out with certain friends? What if they don't let me go back to campus?

I finally turned to look at my mother, who had leaned back against her seat, and to my surprise, had a puzzled look on her face.

"What does that even mean?"

I didn't know whether to laugh or cry, but I tried to explain it to her the best I could. I said, "It means I like people of all genders, not just guys."

She got quiet again. I sat there, wiping away my dry tears and swallowing hard to eradicate the goliath-like lump in my throat.

She asked if it was just a sexual thing. I did my best to clarify that I am attracted to men and women equally, sexually and romantically. At first, it seemed like she was just trying to make sense of this new identity I had introduced to her. Like she was trying to understand her daughter again.

Then, she asked if I was still attracted to boys. I was thankful that she hadn't reacted angrily or with disgust, but at the same time, I was hurt. She was worried, once again, about how people would perceive our family if I only dated girls. Not about the turmoil and the anxiety I was facing while trying to feel accepted.

"Yes, mom, but I am also attracted to girls. This isn't a phase. I want to date girls just as much as I want to date boys."

As my breath caught on my words and the speed of my speech hastened, my mom could tell I was getting worked up. She leaned her head in to look me in the eye.

"I don't see you any differently, and I don't hate you. I still love you, but I have to be honest -- I don't have the courage to protect you from family and friends if you settle down with a girl. I can do it for a friend's child, but it's much more difficult to fight back when it's my own child."

In a messed-up way, it made sense to me. I could trace her logic back to the pressure of community perception. It wasn't ideal, and I wasn't completely satisfied with her response, but it was far better than it could have been. I was so thankful she didn't kick me out or disown me that all I could think to say was, "I'm not going to embarrass you in front of our family or our community. I promise."

She said, "I'm glad you're thinking of us," and that was the end of the conversation. She opened her car door, and we went grocery shopping like nothing happened.

Gossip and judgment in the South Asian community is a vehicle of control. It is best served hot, with a side of chai, and overthrows anything else you might have on the table. So, I accepted the bare minimum my mom had to offer me and settled for tolerance. I shoved all lingering feelings of disappointment and confusion away and did my best to appreciate what she was able to give me.

A few minutes later, we were standing in front of the bread aisle, and she asked me if I was going to tell my dad. I was exhausted from our conversation, and I asked her to tell him.

I heard them through our shared wall that evening talking about it. His response, as expected, was, "I don't care who she marries or what she does as long as she is happy, is not hurting anyone, and is living a life with honesty." That made me smile, and my heart felt warm. I was relieved.

I went back to school the following week with a dedication to get more involved in the queer community. I joined the Queer Trans People of Color (QTPOC) student organization and made an effort to meet more people like me. I started to feel more fulfilled at school, like I finally found my place. But, the more accepted I felt on campus, the more I began to feel uneasy about the half-baked acceptance my mom offered me. I realized that, while I am so privileged to have parents that didn't reject me and still love and support me, this middle ground was confusing and frustrating.

I didn't know how to bring this up to her without it turning into a full-blown argument. So, I didn't. Then, during a weekend I was spending at home, while giddily telling my mom and my brother about QTPOC and the people I had met, I was finally confronted with what I had been trying to avoid. I was excited because I was finally making friends at school -- something I thought my parents would be happy about.

Mom interrupted me. "Are you posting on social media or anywhere that you're bisexual? You're only meeting and talking to these people in person, right?" That was the last straw.

"You don't accept my sexuality. You're ashamed of me." I couldn't hold it in any longer. This time, I wasn't sad or hurt. I was angry.

"Me? You don't understand how much I have compromised for you," she responded.

Hearing that stung. I know how much she's compromised for me -- her beliefs, her time, her energy -- but I compromised a lot for her as well, and she didn't seem to acknowledge that. I forced myself not to pursue romantic relationships with women to protect her from judgment in the community. I was suppressing my identity and beginning to hate myself. I couldn't be myself in public or online because I was worried about what others would think of my mom and our family.

"Mom, imagine if someone from a different race came up to you and said you couldn't do any *Indian* things anymore? You can't do *puja* (prayer). You can't wear *saris*, nothing. Just because they don't agree with your Indian lifestyle. That is what I have felt like. You have asked me to hide part of who I am. I have compromised a piece of me for you."

She stopped to think. It felt like I finally broke through to her.

She said, "I'm going to love you no matter what choices you make and what identities you hold, and I will never be embarrassed by you. It's going to be hard because I grew up believing this was wrong. And I know it's not anymore, but that's still in my head, and it is part of the community no matter how hard I try to think otherwise." I burst into tears again, and this time, I wasn't entirely sure why. Perhaps I was relieved I was able to get everything off my chest or because I finally got the reassurance I needed from my mom to know that she wasn't ashamed of me. It soothed my anger but didn't hurt any less to know my mom might never accept this part of me.

I've had to make peace with the situation. It still bothers me that the reason she doesn't accept my sexuality is not because she believes it is wrong, but because she is afraid of what others will think. I remind myself that I still have her love and that I have people in the queer community to support me no matter what I choose to do in the future.

After that confrontation, I went back to campus and threw myself into activism. It began to feel like the only way to practice my queerness, since I was still hesitant to date women. I worked with other queer friends to prioritize myself and they pushed me to think about my own happiness. I began to realize that in the same way that my mom's happiness resided in the approval of others in the community, my happiness resided in my mom's approval. And that would just perpetuate this toxic chain - it was not sustainable.

It was almost like I went into survival mode; I realized that in order to move forward, I needed to be okay with the fact that my mom accepts me but hasn't fully accepted my sexuality. To be happy, I needed to focus on what I can control - self-acceptance.

I continue to introduce queer television shows and documentaries to my mom, and I think hearing their experiences helps her develop empathy for the queer and trans community. Particularly, seeing the evolution of queer representation in Bollywood (although still not the greatest) has made a big difference in our household.

While the possibility of dating girls still worries me and the idea of coming out to my extended family causes some anxiety, I have decided to focus on the now and worry about consequences later. My relationship with my mom has gotten much better, and my relationship with myself is improving even more. At some point, I hope I do meet a special girl that I can bring home. I don't know when, but I know *jab main use dekha, toh mujhe aisa laga...* (when I see her, I'll feel like…)

Contributor's Bio:

Keerthana (she/her and they/them) identifies as a queer South Asian woman. She was born and brought up in the San Francisco Bay Area in a Telugu family and a large Indian community. Indian culture is a large part of her life, and they are also very involved in advocacy and community work with queer and trans people of color both in the Bay Area and in San Diego, where they attend school. She is an artistic person and loves music (especially the piano) and painting and drawing. They have a very close relationship with their family and friends, and most of their life revolves around supporting them. Overall, she loves people and believes in dedicating her time to improving their quality of life.

Growing up Qatholic

Irene Syriac

as told to Editor

I used to love going to church. Every Sunday at 11:15 AM, you would find my Malayali Catholic family sitting center right at our community church. I would hold onto every word the priest said, truly believing that God was looking out for all of His children and that He loved us, sins and all. Though my priest never directly discussed homosexuality, around 5 or 6 years old, his allusions told me that what I was feeling, my attraction to women, wasn't "normal" according to the church, my community, or society at large.

I still loved going to church, so I folded up my feelings and packed them away somewhere deep in my mind. But every Sunday, sitting there in God's House, I could feel His disappointment in me. Out of all the other sinners filling up the wooden benches around me, I felt like He didn't want me there. I wasn't acting on my intentions, but I felt guilt and remorse for defying His plan.

It was then that I made up my mind to spend the rest of my life celibate, as if that would compensate for all my wrongdoings. I decided that if I could fake being the child He wanted me to be, He wouldn't throw me out, and He might still love me.

During elementary school, I developed my first crush. While I did my best to push it away, this crush lasted for seven years. Yup, you read that right, seven years. At birthday parties in middle school, when girls would stand around gushing over crushes, a random girl would turn to me and ask me who I liked, and I would shrug it off and say, "no one." At some point, I could tell the girls in my class found it weird that I hadn't had a crush for as long as we knew each other, so I picked some conventionally attractive white boy in eighth grade and pretended to be in love with him. My fear of being caught resulted in some severe overcompensating, including commenting on his "chiseled jawline" and "olive skin," whatever that meant.

I ended up attending a Catholic high school. As if my emotions and teenage hormones weren't enough, the school became a terrific breeding ground for self-hatred. I felt so unhappy with myself and was not really sure why. Of course, it could have been many things: being the only South Asian person in an all-white Catholic school, an almost decade of suppressing my sexuality, really, anything.

After writing, thinking, and shedding an Olympic pool's worth of tears, I grew tired of beating myself up. At the start of my junior year of high school, I decided it was time to admit to myself that I have feelings for women. I was still unsure about where I stood in terms of feelings for men, but I was definitely attracted to women. After this monumental revelation, I didn't know what to do next, so I threw myself into whatever forms of media I could find on the matter. I watched movies, read books, and watched countless Youtube videos, but they were all the same. Hypersexualized male gay icons defying the norm and looking good doing it. The few media that I found that included women were all white women, with maybe one biracial woman who looked ethnically ambiguous enough to "diversify" the cast.

The more I explored, the more evident it became that no one understood what I was going through. The unique intersection of being South Asian, Catholic, and queer were nowhere to be found, and I didn't know what the right way to approach understanding myself was. I realized that I had to forge that path for myself and hopefully be that representation for someone else.

The first step was coming out. After graduating, I laid out my plan to do so. I started easy, and with someone I expected would accept me with open arms: my childhood friend, Sheara. Although she grew up in the same religious community, she was so supportive and positive, and it made me feel better not hiding or lying anymore. I continued one person at a time. And, while some went better than others, each pair of open arms opened my eyes to the community that religion had afforded me and, yet, had almost forced me to push away.

I lived at home for my first year at college and, when I finally moved out for my third year, I wanted to make my own decisions. This started with church. I started spending Sundays in the library or with my then-girlfriend. I kept our relationship low key because I had just joined the Indian American Student Association (IASA), and I had some mistrust about coming out in that space. Rightfully so, because after building up my courage to come out to one person in the organization, she told me I was confused.

Confused. I was confused about many things. Did God really care that I was queer or just that I was a good person? Would my parents be more hurt that I lied to them for years or that I was defying their understanding of who I should be? If I lived my truth, would I have to turn my back on the culture and community that raised me?

Suffice it to say, my sexuality was the one thing I was not confused about. But I didn't need to explain that to her. This interaction pushed me out of the South Asian community, and I sought a community that allowed me to embrace my queer identity.

I got involved in social justice theater groups, dated around, and, later, joined an organization for women of color on campus. It was then that I started to feel more comfortable in my identity as being of color and being queer. However, I continued to reject my Catholic identity and failed to understand how that piece fits in with the rest of who I was. There weren't many Catholic South Asians around me anymore, and almost none that identified as being queer. So, I happily grew further away from it.

A few months later, my mom signed me up for a retreat with our Malayali Catholic community. This was an event that we would go to often growing up, but as I began to push back on religion, I was not looking forward to it. I argued with her about having to attend, and we eventually reached a compromise – that I was allowed to leave the retreat early.

When I eventually got to the retreat that Friday morning, I was greeted by, "Irene Mole, you have to meet this Prophet. He is so smart and religious, and he can tell you things about your future and your past that you don't know. Do make time for him." An aunty I grew up with had just met with this Prophet and was gushing over him.

I heard him speak a few times throughout the retreat, often saying things like "We should be grateful for AIDS because it will teach people not to sin" or requiring all of us to hold hands while on our knees praying in a dark room littered with candles. This retreat felt like a cult.

I was getting ready to head home early the next day when the Prophet called me into his private room, where he had held several one-on-ones with other attendees. I was interested to see what he had to say, so I went in and sat with him.

"I can tell you don't want to be here." Now, this wasn't a profound revelation. Anyone with eyes could tell I didn't want to be there.

"Who forced you to come?"

"My mother," I responded.

"You and your mom fight a lot, don't you?" My mom is one of my best friends. We fight maybe once a year, so I could tell this guy was bullshitting.

"Are you dating anyone?"

"No."

"Who hurt you?"

"I'm sorry, what?"

"Are you dating any men?"

"No."

"Are you dating any women?" It occurred to me that he wasn't reading my aura or speaking to God. He was using basic Psychology 101. He asked pointed questions and used my facial and bodily reactions as jumping-off points. I wanted to test him a little to see how he would react.

"Yes, I date women, not men."

He spent the next fifteen minutes ranting about God and homosexuality being a sin and some other expected nonsense. Then, he ended with, "Don't you want to be normal?"

Here's the thing. Anyone who is figuring out their sexuality and is repeatedly told that they fall outside of the norm wants to be normal. I spent my whole life hating myself and being told, directly and indirectly, that I wasn't South Asian enough or wasn't Catholic enough because of this one piece of my identity. So, yeah I wanted to be normal. If he had the power to turn me straight and make me acceptable, I wanted that. Now, I am ashamed that I ever wanted to change, but at the time, I told him "yes."

"I can release you of your bondages. We will exorcise your demons."

Without skipping a beat, he went for it. I sat there, scared and alone, while he intermittently sprayed me with holy water and muttered some prayers under his breath. A few minutes later, he said I was exorcised of my demons and could go. Angry, sad, and confused, I packed up my bags and left.

As soon as I got home, I yelled at my mom about sending me to the retreat. Leaving out some critical details, I told her about the AIDS comment and all the other weird things he had us do. She wasn't offended but seemed confused. This was one of the first times she created space for me to unpack my feelings and openly discuss my views on religion. This was a glimmer of hope.

A couple of years later, after a devastating breakup, I had no one to turn to, and I came out to my mom. She said almost every hurtful thing you could say, but I was so sick of being in the closet that it didn't even matter.

Eventually, exhausted, I said, "I understand that this is uncomfortable for you, and you're experiencing a lot of pain, and this contradicts many expectations you had for me, but I am not doing okay either. I just need to know if I have a home here at the end of the day. That's what I need right now, and if that's not the case, tell me now, and I can go."

She replied, "Of course you have a home here. You will always have a home here. I am just struggling to understand right now, and I am disappointed. But, you always have a home here."

In the conversations we have had since that day, it is clear that her religious side holds her back more than her South Asian side. She is worried about what God will say to her when she gets to heaven. And she is concerned that she failed as a parent in raising me. But, I am helping her work through that, and our relationship is getting stronger as a result.

While I haven't come out to my dad yet, I've made the decision to do it. If there's anything I've learned from my years in Sunday school, it's that God intentionally molds us each in the image of Him. And God makes no mistakes. So, whether I practice Catholicism or not, this must mean that I was placed in this life for a rainbow-encrusted purpose.

My dad has a temper, like most Indian dads. And while my mom thinks he would be more ashamed than angry, and my sister-in-law believes he already knows, I have a feeling he might kick me out. The thought of losing my family is stressful, but it won't stop me from coming out to him. I know that God is looking out for me and has provided me with solid relationships to get me through this.

When my parents moved to this country, they built their support system around Catholicism. I now know how important it is to have a support system, but I don't know if it needs to be based on religion. I'm not as religious anymore in the sense that I don't go to church, and I don't recite those bedtime prayers anymore. But I talk to God a lot. I find Him in nature, in the goodness of humanity, and in my loved ones. While my relationship with organized religion is nonexistent, my relationship with God is strong.

If I could talk to my younger self, I would tell her that her Sundays will be spent making pancakes for her beautiful girlfriend, not at church. I would say not only will she get into the University of Michigan for undergrad, but she will reject Michigan's post-grad offer to move to New York City and pursue a Masters of Social Work. She is going to research the intersectional queer South Asian identity, she will finally be fearlessly proud of this identity, and she will start going to therapy. She is going to fall in love, and her mom is going to like her. And, although Sundays are going to look a little different, she will still be happy, and she will still have a home.

Contributor's Bio:

Irene Syriac (she/her) is an Indian-American born in southeast Michigan. Growing up, she worked in organizations that supported social justice for her community. She attended the University of Michigan for her undergraduate degree in Neuroscience and Women's Studies. Here, she worked directly under the university's president and executive board to create change in its diversity, equity, and inclusion programs. Irene left home to attend NYU's Silver School of Social Work Master's program. In the future, Irene aspires to have her own private practice, to open her own non-profit for LGBTQIA+ minorities, and to teach at a collegiate level. Outside of activism, Irene's interests include theatre, working with animals, and annoying her cats.

part 2:

to those whom i love

Aaria

Ami J. Sanghvi

Every so often, two people collide even when their destinies exist in separate worlds.

She was only a few years away from becoming a full-fledged doctor;

> I was adjusting to life as an author, marketer, and mixed martial artist.

She showed up for our dates with wet hair and uniquely curated outfits;

> I was a fashionista who always had to look my best.

She was born under the most dominant of all water signs;

> My star-alignment was that of infinite flame.

She was timid and shy;

> I was audacious and assured.

It was clear from the beginning that we could never end up together, but still, we neglected our realities; we were both too busy basking under the umbrella of our shared heritage.

We found each other on a dating app, and her profile floored me. The tone of her bio somehow felt effortlessly wise and authentic. Her second photo captured her goofily eyeing down a bagel. Nothing about her came off as pretentious, and it appeared she didn't take herself too seriously. I especially appreciated this since I was quite guilty of taking myself *way* too seriously and generally thrived around people, like Aaria, who made me realize how ridiculous I was by comparison. I thought she was intelligent, interesting, and beautiful. Through our initial virtual correspondence, I quickly discovered her to be kind and funny, as well.

The first time I met Aaria in real life was magical; we rendezvoused at the quirkiest coffee shop and connected in a way I never imagined was possible. It felt as if something mystical was absorbing the rough, dry air of that town, shielding and showering us with ethereal blessings we had yet to understand. We bonded so much so quickly that somewhere between all our laughter and flirting, she opened up about the stresses she was facing. She described the overwhelming pressures and workload of medical school, her strained relationship with her parents who refused to recognize, acknowledge, or accept her queerness, dear friends she struggled to fit into her demanding schedule, and the fact that she was finally ready for a serious girlfriend, but didn't have the time to build a relationship with another person. It didn't help that, living in America, finding other queer South Asian women to date (which she preferred) proved difficult.

Perhaps the statistics are more promising and accurate now than they were a few years ago. Still, back then, most of the national demographic research reported *very* few self-identified sapphics. In that already slim margin, we shared the sentiment that the chances of finding other women with our cultural background felt next to impossible. Our meeting felt like a random miracle; it was clear to us from the beginning that we were the exception, not the rule.

Once the desire for chemistry and compatibility is thrown into the deeply unpromising mix, the likelihood of entering into a long-term relationship with another South Asian woman in the United States becomes nothing more than a pipe dream. At least that's what it feels like.

Aaria and I also agreed on how more often than not, it almost felt easier, as first-generation South Asian Americans, to just give up on the daunting task of trying to find queer companionship for ourselves and become the people society wanted us to be instead: married in our twenties to Desi men with STEM or business jobs and, of course, remaining deeply closeted.

Our first date was so unbelievably successful that it ran from the afternoon well into the evening. By the time we both realized we needed to head home, it was already getting dark outside, and so she insisted on driving me back to my car. Shortly after, we halted at the type of deserted stop sign that neither of us would have felt guilty for prolonging.

This was where I plucked up the guts to ask her if we could kiss.

She smiled and said yes. Thus, I leaned in and, for a few glorious moments, enfolded myself into the welcoming fissure between her lips. We pulled away from each other with astonished sighs; she released a dazed "wow" into the spark-ridden air. For a brief moment, the world was electric, and everything ceased to be real.

A begrudging departure from the stop sign which had stood witness to our first kiss was followed by silly conversations and that type of laughter that can only be birthed in the deepest part of one's gut.

Eager to prolong our time together, she drove slowly, and we indulged in several more inconsiderately long pauses at random stop signs. She would jolt the vehicle to a halt each time, her car our tiny, metal cube of solitude, just so that we could steal a few more fervent kisses from each other.

We reluctantly departed ways at my car, locking lips once again and giggling at each other until we slipped out of each other's sight.

I drove home that night, consumed by dreams and the clutches of twilight's looming darkness.

Life grew so busy that an entire month passed before we were able to see each other again.

The second time we went out wasn't anything like the first. It honestly may have been doomed from the moment I hopped in my car to go see her.

She'd already had a long day before coming to meet me at a location I thought might be clever for our second date: a pumpkin patch and apple orchard I'd discovered during the slowly-chilling folds of mid-October. The crisp air and cooling sunshine seemed like indicators of a beautiful location for a second date with an extraordinary human being.

Unfortunately, my carefully selected venue ended up being quite dull. That mystical something still seemed present in the air on that second outing, but it was different. It appeared diminished, faded as if it was already beginning to give up on us.

We wandered along the corn rows, and our conversation felt forced. The few kisses we dared to sneak had changed since our first date; there was suddenly some invisible barrier forcing us apart, but we both desperately clung on anyway.

We even stumbled upon these peculiarly gigantic pumpkins, and she went ahead and told me all about the condition which caused their sizes. Swiftly, however, the early autumn stomping grounds grew stale, and we agreed to relocate our date to a lounge down the street.

Of course, we both got stuck in the worst kind of traffic on the way there. As a result, we were both wearing more than a bit thin by the time we'd found a table in a dark, dusky corner in that smoky saloon, about an hour later. Our kisses became more flirtatious and eager than they had been earlier, but they still weren't the same as the ones on our first date when it felt like we could never get enough of each other. The spell that had bound us before appeared to be breaking.

We stopped speaking for the most part following this encounter. Her energy towards me had changed since our first date, and after the second, I was doubtful she wanted to see me again. Similar things were occurring on my end. Sensing that having an actual conversation about our feelings would have been just as uncomfortable for her as it would have been for me, I did us both a favor and took a hard exit from her life.

A few more months passed until frost started to waltz across the desolate winter grounds of that wretched town. Her name fondly came to my mind as I overcame the disquiet caused by the girl I'd dated briefly after her, and I knew I had to ask Aaria if she'd have dinner with me. I needed to know if our previous date, the one which had occurred on that stroppy October eve, was just an awkward fluke or if it was an indication of just how badly we fit together.

The curiosity was consuming me; I had to know which of our two previous dates was the real one, even if that meant we never saw each other again after that.

Aaria responded happily to my invitation. Soon after, we reconnected at a delightful little "mom and pop" Italian restaurant, chatting with each other as if no time had passed. It was obvious that the magic in the air was still not as present as it was on the first date. Still, aside from a stressful phone call she received, we had a wonderful time together.

Unfortunately, this time around, she was a bit under the weather, and when we shared our goodnight kiss, she expressed concern about getting me sick. This time, our kiss felt like plain lips on plain lips, unengaged flesh on unengaged flesh; nothing else connected us aside from our physical forms in that unsettling instant. Whatever little was left of that mystical energy had abandoned us.

We'd had a wonderful time together, but we ended that third date with a polite "have a nice weekend" and no expectation of ever meeting again. Perhaps whatever "chemistry" we may have had to begin with was merely a manifestation of the joy we both felt in finding another queer woman from our own background, and perhaps we had just mistaken that for actual compatibility between us. Either way, whatever it was we thought we had shared before was suddenly vanishing before our very eyes. Therefore, without needing to express our mutual discomfort verbally, we relinquished our short-lived romance into the crowded abyss of failed and forlorn love.

A feeling of contentment bloomed within me and remained for weeks to come.

Summer had arrived. Sneaky as ever, the enticing elixirs of our blessed, beaming star had just begun to shower us in its generous warmth, and its glorious, golden hues entirely entranced the world. I was shoulders-deep in my mixed martial arts training; I also had an ongoing correspondence with new, long-distance friends, including a few queer women with whom I was deeply compatible. Aaria felt like a distant memory, a shooting star I may not have beheld in my gaze; I hadn't thought about her much since our third and final date. Things were changing, and I was, too — perhaps even for the better.

Still, her occasional reappearances were becoming a consistent theme in my life, for she came to me once more…

The fourth and final time.

I don't remember the circumstances which brought us to that hotel room. I just remember how anxious I was in the minutes and hours leading up to that final encounter, how there was nowhere else on Earth I wanted to be, and how even from beneath her shy exterior, I could still feel her energy attempting to imbibe me whole. The air between us was more magical, more magnetic than it had ever been before.

I secured the door to our fortress. At long last, our encasement of solitude had expanded from a car into an actual room.

I spun around to gaze at her, this beaming person I couldn't seem to get enough of, and was taken aback by the woman who approached me. She radiated a whitish-gold light. It almost seemed to carry her across the marble floor, closer and closer towards my waiting arms. Her hair wasn't frayed by the stress, toil, agony, and sleep-deprivation of medical school as it usually was; it flowed with ease in what I realized was its natural state…

Dark, long, and sleek.

The shadows which generally overtook her face had vanished, and she wore a smug grin on her face I'd never seen before. Her white silk slip only added to her grace and glory…

She was a woman consumed by the heavens.

Her eyes whispered sweet nothings to me. I reached out to touch her joyous face, and, with her gentle fingers, she adoringly brushed my tresses back behind my ears. The current of her touch startled me, prompting a series of jolts to shock every part of my body and mind. I was dying for what was already occurring:

To be with her at that very moment.

That was when a knock at the door from a hospitality staff member interrupted us. Reluctantly, I opened the door, told them that we needed some time to get settled in, and requested that they return later. Once they agreed to leave us be, I closed the door and turned around again to face the angel in the room.

Something had changed.

Aaria was still just as breathtakingly beautiful as she always was. But, it appeared she'd surrendered that radiance from before in those few abysmal moments I'd looked away. Now, she was sad and confused. Before that interruption, she had briefly forgotten that an entire world existed outside that room; she had experienced a few rare moments of total peace away from a society that never gave her any. Then came that abrupt reminder that forced her to come crashing back down to Earth. Harrowed, Aaria was haunted by her own reality once again.

She spoke in a tired voice. "I think I just want to go to sleep now."

I nodded and proceeded to prepare for bed. I attempted to wash away the electricity of her touch, which still lingered on my skin, in that hotel room sink, but I failed. My skin still endured shocks and jolts, as if her body was still pressed against mine.

There were two queen-sized beds in that suite, and she'd already claimed one of them. She laid there completely still and propped up on her pillows; Aaria was finally beginning to relax again. It appeared she had picked up yet another tinge of brightness, identical to the one from earlier. I found that curious but had no plans to pursue it. As women, we shared a certain degree of understanding and respect, which was more crucial than anything else we could have ever had together. Her happiness was the most important thing.

Aaria raised her hand slightly and beckoned me to lay down next to her. I considered her offer for a moment and then obeyed, feeling confident that she would tell me if she changed her mind and no longer wanted me there.

I made myself comfortable on one pillow, laying flat and as far away from her as I could manage; she was elevated slightly above me, so I rolled onto my side to gaze at her. Her eyes fluttered open, and she, too, turned onto her shoulder so that she could stare back at me. The substance of her soul had overtaken her once again. She'd morphed back into her most angelic form, that version of her that was entirely unburdened by the human world.

There she was. Her skin was nearly as deep in tone as mine; her straight hair and round eyes were darker than the nightfall itself. I was surprised to see how comfortably she wore the exquisite curves of her body, as she generally went through so much trouble to hide them. Her sudden ease was lovely to behold.

I laid there, too. My dark brown hair was long, warm-hued, and curly as ever; my bronze skin glowed just as Aaria's did, and my eyes were even darker than hers.

I wore sweatpants while she wore a gown. Regardless, our moment was still and fated.

I reached out to touch her with an air of apprehension, as I was made nervous by the slight but upward curl of her lips. Encouragingly, Aaria leaned her head forward so that I suddenly found my fingers immersed in the plushness of her ink-colored mane. She lovingly pressed her head into my forearm and grazed it with her lips. Her eyes facing downwards, she smiled with the luminosity of a trillion stars and uttered the words, "This is it: my one true love."

That was a lie, and we both knew it. Still, it didn't bother us. We both seemed to agree that sometimes it's better just to savor the moment before it's gone forever. That night, I felt the same way — like she was my *one true love*, just as I was temporarily hers.

She began to kiss me passionately, and, for a short while, we allowed ourselves to be young, exultant, and madly in love.

I peeled open my eyes the next morning to the sight of Aaria repacking her bag. She was back to her exhausted, aware, and anxious self. I imagine I had reverted to my former, more anguished state by then as well. That glimmer from the night before had already abandoned her. She was in a clear state of alarm again, petrified by the gloom of her own life.

It was as though she sensed I'd woken up; she immediately glanced up to observe me watching her as she hastily packed the t-shirt she had worn the previous day — the yesterday that already felt eons away.

She anxiously zipped her bag shut and ever-so-slowly dragged it off the table; all the while, she held my gaze. Her eyes beseeched forgiveness. In our strained, fragile silence, I granted it to her with my own. It was the right thing to do.

But it also made my chest ache.

Without so much as a final word, she disappeared into the hallway. I remained still as the door snapped shut behind her.

I knew that was the end of it, the end of us. Nevertheless, I didn't try to stop her. I realized even back then that we were far *too* different, surpassing even the notion that "opposites attract" in our undeniable variations. Moreover, we both risked the likelihood that our society would never accept our queerness as South Asian American individuals, let alone as two mismatched, incompatible women in a relationship with one another. Together, we made no real sense — not even to ourselves. But separately, maybe we had a chance.

And then, of course, there were the other factors at play, the ones we can never fully understand. Fate is an enigma; the universe is chaotic, unpredictable, and unfathomable. Sometimes things just happen the way they do for reasons beyond our control.

From all of this, it was clear there would be no fifth encounter between us. Our fourth rendezvous was the charm, and therefore, the final time we would ever be together. It was the end of something, but it was also the eve of the rest of our lives.

I could feel it in my bones.

I tenderly gathered the fragments of her soul, all cast behind her and scattered across the silver-glazed sheets on which we'd loved and slumbered the evening before, and I fed them to the ravenous wind. I sought to give them the chance to find their way back to her someday, to make her whole again. They would be of no use to her trapped in a bundle of silk, and to imprison them in one would've been horribly selfish, despite my dull heartbreak and the corresponding temptation to do so.

Aaria and I left the place behind us as nothing more than an eternal chamber, one which was to be perpetually haunted by those restless apparitions of our squandered love. Even there, a hint of that mystical something lingered in the air.

As I departed the hotel, I thanked God for bringing Aaria into my life, even if only for a few short and heartbreaking encounters, and I expressed my gratitude for that novel gift of hindsight. This wisdom allowed me to conceive how love between humans is supposed to be. Mostly, however, I asked God to free her from all the expectations of our world someday because she deserved to be happy.

We both did.

Contributor's Bio:

Ami J. Sanghvi (she/her) is an Indian-American, queer writer, artist, and MMA fighter. She is an award winning author (Eric Hoffer Book Award finalist) and an M.F.A. candidate. She was also recently published in Awakenings (The Nightingale), For Women Who Roar's e-book "Me Too," The Showbear Family Circus, Rigorous Magazine, Prometheus Dreaming's Prometheus Unbound, Conclave: Outliers by Balkan Press, Asylum Magazine, The Jessie Butler Women's Poetry Contest 100th Anniversary anthology (She Speaks Up!), So It Goes: The Literary Journal of the Kurt Vonnegut Museum and Library, and Inverted Syntax.

Growing up, she moved around enough that she doesn't have an allegiance to a single place, but is now living happily in the Los Angeles area and pursuing her M.F.A. in Creative Writing at the California Institute of the Arts. She is also writing a cross-genre, experimental, mixed media hybrid novel for her thesis, developing her visual art practice, squeezing in video games whenever she can, and living her best goth life.

IG: @eyebrowsandroses || Twitter: @babyvampami || Website: amijsanghvi.com

The Way I Love
Trigger warning: sexual abuse, child abuse

Sarika Persaud, Psy.D.

I have always felt like my love is too much. Sometimes it feels too much for me to hold like my heart keeps pouring and pouring into hands that are hardly cupped. Other times, it feels like my love is too much for others to bear, too intense. I feel like an ocean when they want a quiet pond. I often think that the way I love is too much effort to understand. A question has remained for me over time: Is something wrong with the way I love?

This question has haunted me from a young age. My parents are Guyanese, which means that we visit a small halal butcher shop in Queens Village when we prepare chicken or goat curry. I remember being five or six years old and holding my mother's hand as I walked into the dimly lit butcher shop. The smell was always the first thing that hit me. There was the apparent scent of unbathed feathers and fur, a sharp tinge of blood, and chicken shit -- but behind it all was a smell I could only identify as a mix of terror and mysterious, unknown darkness. The walls were lined with metal cages, packed with frantically clucking chickens. Some were shedding feathers or had furious red patches of skin showing from stress. There was only one fluorescent light behind the distant counter; otherwise, the room was unlit. The floor was white tile, flecked sparingly with dried blood, grey like an old mop had lazily dragged over it. I knew the floor well because I looked down at it most of the time.

I hated being there. I was so frozen and afraid I couldn't even cry. I would see people picking chickens out of cages one by one. I felt helpless and infuriated that I couldn't pick ones just like they did, but to save rather than slaughter. I wondered what gave us the power, in this small, dark room in Queens, to decide which of these beings would die today. My parents, often annoyed at my strong reactions, explained that this was the way of life, that some things need to die for others to live. Other kids knew where meat came from, and they were still happy to eat it. On the other hand, I cared too deeply and loved too intensely.

Who is to say that these animals felt the depth of terror that I was projecting onto them? Who is to say they felt the isolation and helplessness that I thought I connected with? Maybe my need to save them came from an underlying need to be saved.

At around age three or four, I had been sexually abused by a young man whose mother would occasionally babysit me. I couldn't speak about it. I didn't know how. I barely understood what was happening to me, just that it was wrong. But seeing those animals in the butcher shop, hearing the anxious noises they made from being trapped in such close quarters, reflected the trauma of the secret that held part of me hostage. I wanted to show them I noticed them; I saw their fear, and despite how they have been treated, they could be loved. I wanted to feel those things, too.

At nine years old, I discovered Krishna* was my *ishta deva*, or favored deity. In my culture, a favored deity is the God or Goddess to whom you pray the most. They guide you to your higher purpose. I looked to Krishna to teach me how to love and be loved. In different traditions of Hinduism, you arrive at your *ishta deva* by taking on the deity of your family lineage, taking the deity associated with your astrological lunar sign, or by various other means. Mine was different from my mother's, Hanuman*, and I was disappointed. But, I accepted my fate and trusted my guru, or religious teacher, who led me through this ceremony and taught me about Krishna. My guru was handpicked by my parents, as his father was my parents' guru. My guru was a stern man with big glasses and a dark beard. Over time, he softened up considerably and was well-liked by many of his young students. He was funny, engaging, laid-back, and bought us all pizza sometimes.

During the ceremony, my guru took me under a white sheet to tell me my guru mantra, a repeated and pure religious statement. This is done in secret because of the sacred nature of the mantra's transmission. I repeated the mantra daily, dutifully, and found that I started to develop a relationship with Krishna. First, it was a relationship of the mind. I began to study the Bhagavad Gita very deeply and fell in love with how Krishna unfolded knowledge about the nature of the mind and what love is. Then, through fables, I learned that Krishna practiced love as something unlimited, inexhaustible, and accessible at all times. I wanted to be loved just like that, in a limitless, joyous, and profoundly spiritual way.

So, in yearning for that profound love, I began to engage with the people in my life by giving more and more. In elementary school, I drew funny pictures of dinosaurs with sweet messages for friends and left them on corners of looseleaf papers. In high school, I baked big batches of cookies and cupcakes to share with people throughout the day. Even though I considered myself socially anxious, I had no trouble showing my care for others in small and quiet ways.

As I grew older, my desire for a deep, all transforming love manifested into a misconception that being needed was the same as being loved. In South Asian and diasporic cultures, we are taught to sacrifice what makes us feel genuine joy and meaning to serve others and keep others happy and comfortable. I found myself doing exactly this. I sought out people to save instead of mutually fulfilling friendships. I found myself in codependent relationships and in relationships with narcissists, entering into the role of a savior or self-sacrificing lover. In the pursuit of love, I gave my all to people that didn't have as much to give in return.

I wanted to love fiercely, with my entire heart. I wanted to see love as a force that could transform myself and the other person within platonic and romantic relationships. I vowed for this way that I love to be beautiful and boundless. However, I started to realize that not everyone wanted that, at least not in the same way I did. I grew exhausted and empty and alone. I held on so tightly that relationships slipped through my fingers or forced themselves out from my embrace. I loved so hard that people didn't know how to reciprocate. I learned that relationships don't survive if one person is doing all the work or putting the other person back together.

I remember one friend in particular that taught me this lesson. We had been friends since childhood and did almost everything together. We went on vacations together, frequently stayed at each others' houses, and rarely made big decisions without keeping the other in mind. I believed we were as close as time could have made us. But, relationships aren't like flowers that bloom over time. People take more than sunlight and the tick of a clock to open up.

This was true with her. No matter how much I invested in our friendship or in helping her undo toxic relationship patterns, her walls were firm and guarded. I tried hard to read the sadness and anger on her face but could never quite figure out what was going on in her mind. I always saw love as an exchange of support, but I couldn't be completely vulnerable with her when she refused to let me in. The more I tried to break her open, the more she pushed me away. I was pouring myself into an empty cup and depleting all I had to offer, without realizing that she didn't want to, nor did she need to, change.

Our relationship eventually fell apart, and I felt hollow. Disappointed and hurt, I was convinced there had to be something wrong with the way I love.

I came up against walls with others over and over because I expected them to want to give and receive love the way I did. When their boundaries and needs were different than mine, I was confused. Eventually, these heartbreaks taught me that not everyone wants a love that is as deep as mine. Not everyone wants a love that transforms them. I believed that every relationship should be filled with love that increases our capacity for compassion, helps us heal from past pain, and catapults our growth. But, people give love and receive love at different frequencies and in their own time. It is not my job to bring people to the level that I am at, nor is it fair to expect others to match my frequency.

I have this understanding now, but at the time, I perceived their refusal to let me in as rejection and retreated into myself. Shutting down in this way seemed like a protective mechanism. Over time, I have come to learn that closing your heart at the taste of perplexity is often a natural response to trauma.

When adults face a traumatic event, they often engage in the typical fight-or-flight response. However, children and adolescents do not always have the emotional capacity to escape in that way. They tend to attach to a caregiver for support. But when the adult in their life that they look to for support is also the source of abuse, this can be confusing and deeply damaging. This was certainly the case for my relationship with my guru. My parents often forgot to plan things for my birthday. It made me feel alone, but I quickly became used to feeling forgotten. One year, when I was a teenager, my guru asked me what my parents had gotten me for my birthday. I felt embarrassed but told him that they hadn't gotten me anything. He was quiet for a few seconds after I said that and looked sad.

He seemed genuinely hurt and taken aback and immediately took me out to get ice cream. It was moments like these that I look back at with confusion: I felt deeply loved and cared for, and yet, can also recognize that he may have been preying upon my emotional weaknesses to foster my trust.

When I was sixteen, my guru secretly began to abuse me sexually. It started on my first trip to India and lasted until I turned twenty. It warped my perception of love and terrified me into recoiling from the people and things I loved. I found escape in reading and, later, the arts. I painted, played sitar, and learned Hindustani vocals. I committed to *Bharatanatyam*, and later, to *Kathak*. My art excelled, and my paintings were beginning to show in galleries. I refused to talk about my art, though. If art was an expression of my love, that meant that it was inherently damaged.

I started to distance myself from my guru. The mantra that he had given me began to feel corrupted, somehow. I still loved Krishna, but whenever I tried to chant the mantra, it felt less potent. It also brought back uncomfortable feelings and anxieties for me. I hated that a man like him could get in the way of my relationship with Krishna. I continued to try to connect with Krishna through singing and dance, which mostly worked. However, because of my growing disdain for whatever creative work came from inside of me, I could only fully enjoy these things in private and had great difficulty with feeling worthy enough to share my art with others. It was then that I decided to embody Krishna's values and love in the work that I do instead of the art that I create.

I became a psychologist. My sense of others' struggles gave me strong intuition in this profession. Therapy came easy to me. I was surprised at how quickly I could connect and gain rapport with people who had the highest walls up. Even people with very strong paranoia or delusions found themselves quickly feeling comfortable with me. Overall, while I was rigorous in my study of psychotherapy techniques, I noticed that what helped my clients was being listened to, the feeling of being seen. A feeling that also helped me work through my traumas when I attended therapy. Without words, I wanted them to know that they deserved to feel love, just for who they are. It was fascinating to see how open my clients were to the power of love to heal and transform them, albeit within the bounds of psychoanalytic love.

But the therapeutic relationship, the ability to use love to heal, is not the same as love in other relationships. My patients appreciated me but never really knew me. As I grew older, I craved deeper relationships, mutuality, intimacy. I started to be more conscious about who I spent my time with and found myself feeling comfortable with other artists and writers, especially in the South Asian classical arts scene. Our relationships not only bloom out of common interests but also out of a common need to recognize deep, intense feelings. Finally, I started to feel that maybe I was not "too much." I told this to my dear friend Mohit, a *Kathak* dancer, one day.

He said, "Let me tell you something -- the way you love is the way humanity should have loved each other forever. We would have been in a beautiful world if we did. The unfortunate reality of so many of us is that we have been conditioned to block off love. You help me to open up my heart to accept and give without getting caught up in endless cycles of expectations and jealousy. That feeling is one of liberation."

I never lost touch with the intensity of my inner world. I was happy to find people who not only shared the same emotional fullness but who were eager to understand what I held within myself as well. I started to meet a part of myself that knew, intrinsically, that my heart was big, full, and had limitless love to give. If by nature, love is infinite, then it cannot be diminished no matter how much you share with others.

I still feel connected to Krishna. I want to continue to love the way he loves – openly, freely, without bounds, but always from a place of genuine respect and dignity for self and the other. He dances with all and none. He is unafraid of showing how much he loves. With one glance, he exudes the limitlessness of compassion in his heart – limitless, because he can never tire of giving it. Very few of his relationships, even friendships, ever fit any sort of mainstream social boundaries – and he felt no shame about that. He was what he was, and he sought the company of people who loved him for that.

Sometime later, I found myself falling in love with someone -- but I wasn't ready to admit that to myself quite yet. We danced around his living room one summer evening. I wanted to dance closer to him but knew that I would have to bear witness to all that my heart felt if I got too close. Being near him felt like a magnet for all of the love that wanted to pour out of me. I wasn't quite sure yet how he would receive it. I noticed every little thing about him, no matter how mundane or strange. I loved how serious he looked while dancing. It made me laugh -- not because he danced in a funny way, but because he was so intentional about the way he moved, even while casually swaying about. He reminded me of an old film star getting a feel for some choreography before a film shoot. I felt like I was losing my mind, being so comfortable dancing around his living room like that, noticing the way a curl of hair fell onto his forehead just so. A thought crept up my neck as I saw the sun begin to set outside his window: If I was to submit to this madness, I wanted to do it with him.

We tired quickly that night. We had already finished a bottle of wine, and we had guests over earlier for his birthday. He slumped back onto the couch, and I reclined next to him. I gazed intently at the small black dot at the base of his right thumb, and I thought about how it was one of the most beautiful things in the world. I asked him what music he wanted to hear. He said, "Something by S.D. Burman."

At that moment, I was transported back to my grandfather's living room. I spent much of my childhood in their home off of Fordham Road in the Bronx, as my parents would leave me there for large stretches of time in the summers. I remembered one evening when his living room smelled like a freshly poured glass of whiskey. Everything was awash in dim, orange light from the lamps in the corners of the room, blending in with the sepia and dull gold furniture. Their decor was decidedly very 70's, frozen in time for as long as I knew them. My grandfather was obsessed with S. D. Burman, and on this night, had a song of his performed by the inimitable Mohammed Rafi playing from the record player: *"tere mere sapne ab ek rang hai."* ("Now, your dreams and mine are of the same color.")

My grandfather would hold my little hands and slowly waltz me around the living room. I was probably five or six years old in this memory, barely at his waist height. He would always sing along in his distinctive accent, somewhere between a formal British accent and a typical West Coast Guyanese creole. I would feel shy after a minute or so and run to sit on a chair near the window, the sound of the above-ground four trains rumbling past.

He would then bring my grandmother to dance with him, even if she was finishing up cooking in the kitchen. She was always, always laughing in her gleeful high-pitched melody. My grandmother was short and had wild, curly hair, just like I did at that age. She reminded me of a beautiful little bird. My grandfather loved the actor Dev Anand, who featured in the movie *Guide*, where this song was from. He would hold my grandmother close and do a sort of freeform waltz with her as the record played, all of the while trying to mimic Dev Anand's signature squint and smile. My grandmother would laugh and laugh.

In the present, I had no idea if he reciprocated the love I felt, but I felt at peace knowing that I had memories of the type of love that felt healthy, whole, and good. I remembered my grandparents, two people, full of joy in themselves and choosing to share life in the most authentic way they could.

I'm learning to accept that to me, love means freedom. The more I unlearn my past traumas and cultural expectations, the more I can turn that love outwards in a healthy way. My capacity to love can not continue to shrink or swell to make others comfortable. Instead, I need to avoid relationships that aren't good for me and relax into myself, learning to be satisfied with who I am. I can focus on turning my awareness inwards while holding the other person accountable, rather than directing all of my energy towards them. I can build an understanding of how others' expectations may have impacted how I hide or express my love, and I can slowly and steadily peel away that which does not serve me. Ultimately, though the way I love affects others, my love is my own. And it is perfect just the way it is.

Contributor's Bio:

Sarika Persaud, Psy.D. (she/her) is a psychologist based in New York City. Her work focuses on destigmatizing mental health help-seeking, suicide prevention, and sexuality and relationships in the Indo-Caribbean and South Asian communities. Sarika is the Coordinator of Diversity, Inclusion, and Social Justice Initiatives at Fordham University (Lincoln Center campus), and is an adjunct professor in the Master's program at CUNY John Jay University. Sarika is also a Kathak dancer and a poet.

Swing

Shaji Mathews

Disclaimer: This story is about internalized homophobia, biphobia, classism, and racism that the contributor fought/fights within himself, influenced by his society, friends, and family. Therefore, this piece includes connotations of classism, racism, and biphobia in reflecting on these problematic ideas. These views are not encouraged by the author of this story or the editor of this anthology. This piece encourages readers to think about their views on race, class, color, and sexuality and how they might manifest in their interactions with others.

Gabriel said he needed to take a break from me. Anna Maria Consuela Gonzalez, the lady he met at the church a month ago, came over to his place the night before for drinks. Apparently, one thing led to the other. The next morning, they woke up to the crisp Michigan spring and walked over to the neighboring elementary schoolyard. According to Gabriel, they sat on a swing and swung like two children.

"You know Papi, as much as I like you, the two of us can't sit on a school swing like that," he said. I knew that was true. I wasn't ready to sit on a swing with him in a schoolyard.

Gabriel was my on-and-off lover for the past six months. He was bisexual and made no bones about it. So, to me, it was a given that he could fall off the gay wagon at any time. I hoped it would last longer.

We met at the gym. He was lifting weights with ease but not with the dedication of those gym rats. He took time to chat with folks, laughed, cracked jokes, mostly in Spanish. I didn't understand most of it but still found the full-throated laughter exciting. He did turn to me once and asked, *"Que pasa?"* ("What's up?") for which I could not come up with a quick enough response. He caught up with me in the steam room after the workout.

"How are you, Papi?" he asked.

"Bien," ("Good") I replied in the limited Spanish I had.

"Did you have a good workout?" He asked.

I said, "yes, but I wish I could lift weights like you."

"You know Papi," he said, "You have the perfect little body. Why do you want to bulk up? You are hot as is." I blushed. He thought I was hot!

Gabriel invited me out for a beer. We went to a local Latino bar where everyone knew him. Some guys came up and spoke to him in Spanish, occasionally glancing at me and saying something that I didn't understand. All through, Gabriel had his arms wrapped around me like we had been pals forever. The hair on his forearms rubbed against my bare shoulder that was left uncovered by my sleeveless workout shirt. He would pull me in once in a while after a joke with the bartender or another patron that resulted in a burst of heavy laughter. He still had a mild sweat smell mixed with the liquid soap fragrance from the gym shower. His fingers played drums on my shoulder to the music from the jukebox when we were just sitting sipping our beer.

Gabriel grew angry only once that evening. I wasn't sure exactly what happened, but a guy walked over to us and took a glance at me before saying something to him in Spanish. I heard Gabriel telling him off with some harsh words, all the while tightening his arms around me nonchalantly. We left the bar soon after. I followed Gabriel's pickup truck in my car all the way to his home.

Gabriel lived in a trailer park. I was afraid to park my Audi in front of his mobile home, but he assured me that his friends, *"amigos"* he called them, would make sure no one messed with "Gabriel's guest's car." Once we were inside, clothes came off in no time at all. Air conditioning was barely functioning in the closed-up mobile home, and sweat poured out of our bodies and mingled.

Gabriel's walls were covered with pictures of his former life with a girlfriend and a child they had together. She moved back to Mexico with the child, and he didn't know where they were. He was with that girlfriend for only three years, but it sounded like they were together for a lifetime.

"Do you miss her?" I asked. "I don't miss her so much as missing the times we had, Papi," he replied. The times they walked around the town, when they went to church together, when they had been to friend's houses or parties as a couple.

I knew he had to go to work early the next morning, so staying over was not in the cards. And I didn't expect it to be more than a one evening affair anyway.

But we kept seeing each other. Saturday night sleepovers at his place and Sunday morning breakfast with huevos rancheros followed. Weeks led to months.

Some Sunday mornings, I had to leave Gabriel early so he could go to church for the mass in Spanish. There was socializing afterward. Sometimes that led to invitations to parties for someone's birthday or anniversary. That was his world, and I was not part of it, nor did I want to be. On those days, I wandered the streets aimlessly or went to the movies to watch something brainless. If he was not too late or not too tired, he texted me to come over, and I jumped in my car and drove ten miles to spend a half-hour with him. On those nights, he would reek of cigars and cigarettes from whatever party he went to, even though he didn't smoke, and other miscellaneous smells he picked up from the people he hugged or kissed on the cheeks. I would close my eyes and seek his musk beneath all that. His speech would be slurred, but no less passionate, when he uttered my name and called me Papi. "Did you have a good time?" I would ask, for which he would cover my mouth with his as if that was the answer. His breath would smell of Mexican cheese.

Was I falling in love with Gabriel? I wasn't sure, but I fantasized aloud about us moving together into a nice house in a nice suburb. My computer software job paid well enough to take care of the mortgage. We would adopt a puppy from the shelter, one of those abandoned things that look at you with pleading eyes in the rescue shelter commercials. I didn't want some silly Pomeranian or Shih Tzu, but a Golden Retriever or a German Shepard, a dog that would make me proud when I took him out for a walk in the neighborhood. Gabriel wanted a Chihuahua, but I wasn't having any of that. Of course, other than the dog, he didn't express any interest in discussing our future suburban life. He said it would not work. "Why not?" I would ask. "We live in different worlds, Papi," was his response.

I couldn't invite Gabriel to my apartment too often. I was afraid of us running into one of my friends. Most of my gay friends had a certain expectation about their boyfriends or dates, and Gabriel didn't fit that mold. While he was healthy and well built, he wasn't built like a model, nor did he dress like one. And he was older than me. And darker. Skin tone still meant a lot to the post-colonial Indians.

Introducing him to my family was out of the question as well because I wasn't out to them. My parents in New Jersey were still waiting for me to find the *right* girl with the *right* credentials to get married. They periodically threaten to find one for me through "the Indian connections" if I waited much longer. I had been using the excuse of my busy career. Many of my desi gay friends were in the same boat. We were all living multiple lives: there was the professional life and the associated social life where everyone knew that I was gay and didn't care; the Indian social set (read: straight) that I mingled with for celebrations such as *Diwali* and *Holi*; and the mainstream gay life which revolved around bars, clubs, and parties.

In reality, Gabriel didn't fit into any of these lives. None of my Indian gay friends or even my parents, if they ever accepted my sexuality, would have considered him to be a catch. But, in my fantasy house in the suburb where I lived with Gabriel, none of that mattered.

Everybody I knew showed up for our fabulous parties. I even picked out napkin rings in rainbow colors at the Provincetown store during summer vacation.

Gabriel couldn't go on vacation with me. For one, his job as a landscaper offered him no paid vacation. And he didn't really want to hang out in a "gay place like Provincetown," according to him. And what about my friends who I was sharing a house with on the beach?

On occasion, when he came to visit me in my apartment, his beat-up pickup truck stood out in the parking lot. "Not a residence but a lifestyle," my place proclaimed on their billboards. Most tenants were professionals driving expensive cars and wearing brand-name clothes. On weekends when Gabriel had to work an extra shift in the afternoon, he sometimes stopped by for a short visit. I would open the building door and let him into my place as quickly as I could without uttering a word in the corridor. Many of the neighbors were not necessarily friends, but acquainted enough to say "hi" in the hallway or receive a package from UPS for each other. There was no hiding the fact that I was gay, nor did it seem to matter to them. But, something in me didn't want the neighbors to see me with Gabriel.

The nights Gabriel came over, he was tired from work but perked up after a kiss and a beer. His touch awakened me every time. My lips savored every part of his body. He rarely spent the night as he had to go to work the next day or church if it was the weekend.

Last month, on a Saturday night, Gabriel told me he would be going to church the following morning. It was the festival of Mary of Guadalupe. After church, there was the usual formal gathering with coffee and donuts followed by informal mingling. Gabriel met Anna Maria Consuela Gonzalez, who came to church with her nana. Nana was from the same town as Gabriel back in Mexico. Anna Maria's grandmother invited Gabriel over for lunch at her place. Anna Maria was new in town and needed to find a place to live. "Would you drive her to a few places to check out?" Nana asked Gabriel.

I didn't see Gabriel for several days. Gabriel told me about meeting Anna Maria at the church and driving her around apartment hunting in the next few evenings. She smelled good, this much he told me the next day. Somewhere along the way, Anna Maria started holding on to his free hand resting on the seat between them, and he didn't let go. The lady who was subletting her basement wanted to know if Gabriel would be staying with Anna Maria and they both said "no" at the same time. The lady said it's ok if they wanted to, that they made a cute couple, Gabriel told me. Gabriel spent several evenings helping set up the new dwelling for Anna Maria.

It had been thirty days since the church festival when Gabriel told me he needed to take a break from me. When I got to his place that evening, instead of lounging in bed waiting for me to undress as usual, he was sitting on the couch. Gabriel told me about the previous night's sleepover and the morning with Anna Maria on the swing.

"Papi," he said, "I miss being part of a couple and doing 'couple things' like sitting on the swing."

I looked up at him.

"Aren't we a couple?" I asked. "What do you want, Gabriel? Want to move someplace together? I can find a job in another city where no one knows us."

He looked at me. "You know that won't work," he said. "*Papi*, our worlds are different."

I got up, laced my shoes, and left. The last thing I heard was the television clicking on and soccer on Telemundo behind the closed door.

As much as I knew and expected this end, all through my drive home, and later, I kept looking for something to cling to. All I found in my apartment was the yellow toothbrush that I offered him the first time he spent the night at my place.

Contributor's Bio:

Shaji Mathews (he/him) is a gay male born and brought up in Kerala, India. Until his mid-twenties, he brushed his gayness aside as a passing phase. Being brought up in a Catholic family left him with a lot of guilt to deal with. When he decided between marrying a woman under societal pressure and continuing to live in India or moving to the USA under the pretense of a better career, he chose the latter. He finally accepts himself as who he is, has come out to his family and friends, and has found love. He has reached out to other South Asian LGBTQIA+ folks over the years and co-founded Trikone Michigan in 1996. His immigrant angst paired with the internalized homophobia, classism, and racism he fights every day within himself led to this story's creation.

One Broken Heart Closer

Trigger warning: suicide

Nandini Roy

16, Drunk, She was straight

"But, I bet you'd never kiss me."

I looked up at her sheepishly. And when I didn't lean in, she did. There we sat, on a white bench in the gazebo upon my still lake. Still, like us. Still, except for my hands in her hair. Still, except for my thumping heart.

Our first kiss was deep and sweet, partly from serious inebriation. I felt safe, mostly, with an encroaching fear of what might happen should my parents wake up. She looked up at me with deep brown eyes, and all worries ceased. This time I leaned in.

Her tongue made its way out of my mouth and across my neck. I felt her edge lower and lower, and my hand mirrored on her body. I felt the goosebumps on her arm and the rip in her leggings and, soon, I felt her.

This wasn't just my first time having sex with a girl. This was my first time.

Was I doing it right?

Do I look as good with my clothes on the floor as I did with them covering the stretch marks on my thighs?

Am I moaning correctly? Am I moaning at the right intervals?

Does she want to be doing this? She's straight. Why is she doing this? Is this my fault?

I looked down at this girl wrapped in a blanket, undressed. My best friend. My very heterosexual best friend.

At that moment, I realized that I, tragically, truly did love her. And she probably didn't feel the same way. But my body didn't give me time to think about how miserable that would make me in the near future. I wanted her more than I had ever wanted anything before in my life. Every fiber of my body was screaming at me to stop stalling, to pull this girl against me as tightly as I could and never let go.

And I did. We knocked over beer bottles with our bare feet and erupted in girlish giggles when one plopped into the water. We explored each other's bodies like experts. I gazed at her dimly lit face in the moonlight and wanted nothing more than to make her mine.

Then, morning came.

Not sure of how to handle the situation, I offered her a shirt and breakfast inside. We showered - separately - and she went home. We tried to unravel what happened many times, but we could never find the words to describe what we wanted the night to mean. She wasn't ready to define herself, and I didn't want that definition to cost me her. Before long, our many failed dates and inconspicuous hand-holding, hastily pulled apart when we ran into someone we knew, dissolved whatever might have been.

It ended as abruptly as it began. We held onto our friendship and decided that was best for us. Maybe it's better this way, but I think about that night often. I think about the warmth of the blanket and the softness of her lips. I remember the hush of the water and the clinking of bottles. I remember every detail so vividly, and I don't think I have ever felt quite so alive.

18, Cold, She was brilliant

"Tell me more."

It was bitingly cold in the middle of winter. My first time living in a snowy city, I was clearly not prepared in an impractical grey long sleeve shirt.

I was a freshman in college, living in dorms that required a key card to enter and exit buildings. She was visiting a mutual friend and brought her service dog Audio with her. Audio resembled a handful of popcorn in puppy form - white, fluffy, and filled with contained energy. Whenever she suffered one of her depressive episodes, Audio was trained to support her by barking or bringing her medication. That evening, I accompanied her as she took Audio out to pee, under the guise of offering my key card for building access. I made the most of this opportunity to get to know her.

We spoke about race and politics and her conservative, religious upbringing. I learned about the mile and a half she would bike every day to her local library to take out forbidden books, including Harry Potter and political commentary, and stood in awe of her hunger for education. I bit my tongue to bear the freezing tundra, holding on to every word she said for warmth.

We exchanged numbers and texted on and off for months. We communicated in memes and emojis and shared passions, music, and dreams. We disagreed over the value of a diamond ring versus the experience of a globe-trotting honeymoon, and she opened my eyes to a life outside of my bubble. A life I had never thought of, free of belongings and dollars, but rich in travel and culture. I grew to yearn for this world.

In our last conversation, she was planning a road trip to visit me while I took summer classes. She was going to drive to her sister's place, stop by a couple of art museums, and park in the always-half-empty lot near my freshman year dorm.

The next day, I heard the news through our mutual friend. She was heaving through tears, gesturing to me to come closer. I was frozen, scared. I didn't want to know how it happened. I didn't want to validate the reality of this loss.

The obituary talked about the light in her eyes. I thought about the way those eyes glistened when she cracked a bad joke or described a career practicing bioethics. It went on to describe the loving family she would be leaving behind. I thought about the mother that abandoned her daughter when she discovered she was gay. The obituary said she dimmed the light herself, but my heart told me it was stolen by a culture that couldn't celebrate her the way she deserved.

I remember flying home that summer, gazing down at the cotton candy sky and the buildings that looked like legos and the people that looked like ants. I wondered if she could see the world the way I saw it at this height. I thought about what it would be like to fall. Not to jump, but to fall. An accident that would take me to her and allow us to recreate that world we dreamed about. Amidst it all, I stayed in my seat. I thought about the pain of losing her and never wanted to perpetuate that. I thought about the life she had ahead of her and wanted to live that for her. I thought about the diary entry I kept in my jacket pocket, and I re-read it to soothe myself to sleep.

"I wish I could describe the impact you had on my life, even for a brief period. And the impact you had on the people I love. When I think of my friends, my parents, my blessings, I know you sent them for me. You made me feel interesting. And you, my God, you were interesting. You deserved so much more, and I am so sorry we could not give that to you. You dared to push the boundaries of what you know. You could have changed the world. And I hope you still can. I miss you. I'm sorry."

21, Eager, She wasn't ready

"Maybe this is it, then."

I lay in bed that night, clutching my chest, praying the pain away. I've heard people dramatically talk about heartbreak before. The cathartic, night-long cries. The unbridled and sporadic bitter anger. The replaying of every fight and disagreement, attempting to piece together where it all went wrong. Why I wasn't good enough. As fury fizzled into exhaustion, the whistle of the wind brushing against my window lulled me to sleep.

I woke up in the morning and had to resist the urge to call her, like a morbid flashback to reality. I thought about the first time we met. On top of a Garden of Eden-esque mountain in the Pacific Northwest. She was glazed in heat and washed in honey, staring through her camera lens to catch the rainbow as it refracted off of the water below us. So focused on getting the perfect shot, she didn't notice me staring.

I thought of the months we spent together, and I wondered how much of it was a romanticized reality. When all-night FaceTimes transformed into missed calls, was there nothing left to talk about, or were there things we preferred not to say? When we jumped into a routine that took forever to label, did we move too fast or not fast enough? I punish myself for willfully ignoring the signs my friends warned me about.

The next day, when I finally made it out of bed, I dragged out the drawer I cleared for her things and neatly folded her sweaters and jeans into a spare box. I try to maintain my composure as the lady at FedEx charges me exorbitantly to ship her belongings across the country. As I walk back home, past that coffee shop we went to on her first weekend visiting me, I choke on memories and inside jokes that seemed too good to be true and bite my lip to hold myself together.

I recall the seven-minute call that broke us apart, revealing the decaying roots we ignored for so long. The distance was hard. The pandemic confused things. Where would our futures take us? Was it worth sticking together to figure out? Neither of us proposed solutions. We sat in silence, expecting the other to make a move. I expected her to fight for us, and it seemed like she expected me to let her go. When the absence of movement and sound overwhelmed me, she won.

My mother called me the next week, and I put on my best smile and described a day so disgustingly happy and productive that she doesn't question my days of silence. My body stiffens with every lie, and I ache to pour myself into my mother's lap. I wish for her fingers to comb through my hair as she hums Kishore Kumar and tells me it will all be okay. But I can barely admit to myself what I allowed this heartbreak to do to me, let alone admit it to my mother. I tell her I love her and end the call.

I throw my phone across the room and cup my forehead in my palms. I think about this powerful and beautiful connection that burned so bright; it indeed did burn. I think about how easily she walked away, seemingly unscathed.

I think about what it would feel like to hurt her the way she hurt me. Then, I think about what it would mean to love her the way she needed to be loved. An all-encompassing love to fill up all the pieces of her that were broken.

Months go by, and I wonder what it would feel like to love again. I wonder what it might take to forgive her. I go on some really good good dates and some really bad bad dates. I fall in love with going on walks and talking to friends and, slowly but surely, the pain dissipates, and my heart feels whole again.

23, Single, She is happy

"One day…"

I remember sitting on my couch with the window open one spring evening. The sun was setting and the wind danced against the gemstones that hung on the windowpane. I was reading a book; I don't remember the name, but I remember looking up and thinking to myself, this is a perfect moment. I could feel it in my bones.

My whole life, I have always planned for perfection. I am a *list* person. I make lists about what I want my dream apartment to look like, what qualities I want my soulmate to have, what I want my life at 30 to look like. I imagine that these lists will bring me to perfection, to happiness. However, that moment, that unscripted moment, was more perfection than I could ever plan for.

I am learning that these lists aren't reality. I let myself make these lists because they make me feel secure. I make these lists because I worry that I allow perfection to slip through my fingers if I don't. But, life has a plan of its own. It creates happiness for me if only I let myself find it.

One day, I'll find that true partner, that best friend, that soulmate. I'll find someone that makes me laugh and makes me feel interesting and who will fight for a love like ours.

In the meantime, I will find happiness in the little things. I will drink coffee by my window and space out to the chirping of Chickadees. I will spend hours in the mountains, hiking with acquaintances and friends. I will take bubble baths on Sundays and think about nothing. I will find a family in a new city and never forget that perfect moment.

Maybe I'll find love, and maybe it will hurt if it ends, but maybe that is just one broken heart closer to happily ever after.

Contributor's Bio:

Nandini Roy (she/her) is a recent college graduate with a passion for social justice. Her interests include traveling, reading, and cooking. Nandini has written and performed many pieces about the experiences of being a woman of color during her college career. As of recent, she has been exploring her intersecting identities of being South Asian and LGBTQIA+. This is her first time writing about her past relationships with women, and she hopes it inspires others to see past heartbreak to something beautiful, another chance at happiness.

part 3:

to the society that raised me

Dancing Between The Good And Bad

Trigger warning: mention of suicide, homophobic slurs

Mr. Patel

as told to Editor

I am a good dancer. Scratch that, I am a great dancer. I remember sneaking out to the parties that the closeted founder of a popular local beverage company would throw at his farmhouse for the gay community in Pakistan, just to show off my moves. One night, I was in the middle of the dance floor, surrounded by a circle of people clapping and cheering me on, while I strutted to "It's the Time to Disco," blaring through the speakers. It felt so good to be amongst the queer community in Karachi and, for the first time in a while, to feel normal and supported for being me.

Then, gunshots.

People scattered and screamed. The music stopped and all I could think was, "run." I jumped out of the nearest window and, on the other side of the fence, I saw a row of police officers raising their guns into the air and firing them. I saw the officers use sticks to beat party attendees. I saw them grab guests by the ankles and drag them across the street, scratching their chests and staining the ground with blood.

I ran as fast as I could, past the officers, and into the field. I saw blinding headlights approaching me from the right, momentarily blinding me. The car stopped next to me, and the door opened. I peered in, cupping my hand over my forehead to shield my eyes from the light. To my relief, a kind gay couple greeted me and offered to drive me home. I couldn't fathom the words to thank them, but their selfless support saved my life that night.

The queer community in Karachi is a connected, loving, and helpful one. The hatred we received from larger society forced us to form our own hidden community, and that might be why we are so close-knit. We look out for one another; kind of like a chosen family.

I got home at 4AM and found my furious older brother waiting for me in the living room, legs sprawled and arms crossed, seated in the center of the couch.

After coming out to my mother the previous year, and receiving questions about whether it was, in fact, an issue with my ability to reproduce, she encouraged me to come out to my brother. I hesitated, telling her it was too soon and that he wouldn't understand. She eventually walked me over to his room and forced me to out myself.

There was an awkward silence for a moment. He looked down, looked away, and then looked back at me.

"This is because of the bloody *faggots* you hang out with." He spit.

The conversation ended there. I understood that it was an influence of the conservative society in Pakistan and that it was an identity he had never really been exposed to and couldn't relate to. Maybe he just needed some time, I thought. But, as the older brother in our family, he had an inevitable dominance over me.

My brother went on, "He is going to spoil the image of our family. He is setting a bad example in the community. Ground him to protect him from fornication and for his safety. An embarrassment."

He locked me away in my room, only allowing me to leave to attend the classes I needed to complete my Radiology degree. I was miserable and lonely, so I turned to *Orkut,* a social media platform. After getting comfortable on this page and finding a kind of refuge among the people, I created a group called YTOP. The acronym didn't stand for anything specifically and I had no real expectation for the group other than fostering safe connections for the Pakistani gay community. News of this group quickly spread through the gay community in Pakistan and, soon, hundreds of men across the country were creating fake profiles to hide their identity and meet other men who understood what they were going through. Through this community, I gathered email addresses and began communicating with these men. They began disclosing their locations to me and I started connecting gay men who lived in close proximity to each other. The group grew from virtual connection to physical community.

During the time that I was locked away, my only escape was the nights I was able to sneak out to the founder's parties. There, I met many of the men I had connected with online, and I learned about the impact that connecting with each other through *Orkut* had had on their lives. There was a man who was about to commit suicide because he felt so alone and ashamed after running away from his forced marriage to a woman, but after reaching out to another gay man in his area, he was able to find a place to stay and seek refuge. There was another man whose father chained him to a chair after finding out he was gay, only allowing him to move to use the bathroom or to eat. A man he connected with through this group offered to pay his father off and save him from that life. It was amazing and heartwarming to see that simply connecting people with similar identities and struggles offered them the life-saving resources and caring community they needed to survive.

This is why, when I got home the night of the party, and felt the wrath of my brother's anger and disgust, it didn't faze me as much, because I knew I was doing something important. Even if he didn't understand this now, one day he would see that I am not an embarrassment, and I am worth something.

I listened to what he had to say and turned around to walk to my room. As I opened my bedroom door, I heard him snicker.

"So, if you're really gay, do you like to give or receive?"

I shut the door and laid on my bed, eyes wide open staring at the ceiling fan. You see, I'm a *side*. Outside of the typical gay culture binary of "tops" and "bottoms" lives "sides." I do not enjoy or require anal penetration when it comes to physical intimacy. I enjoy touching, fondling, oral play, rimming, and many other kinds of sex that are not penetrative. There are so many ways that I experience intimacy, emotionally and physically, beyond this type of sex, but that makes it a complicated identity for other gay men to comprehend, let alone a straight man with no respect for the LGBTQIA+ community. So, I stayed quiet, and tried to get some sleep.

A few months later, my mom announced that it was time for her and my father to move to the US to complete their immigration process. My older brother, already 21, wasn't eligible to immigrate with us since he wasn't legally a dependent anymore, so it became my responsibility to move with my parents and look after them.

I remember sitting in the airplane, crying as we embarked, because I didn't know what my life in the US would look like. After calling many admissions offices, it turned out none of my qualifications or degrees would transfer and I would have to start from scratch. I had no friends and no concept of what the LGBTQIA+ community in the US would be like. All I had heard was that it was more "open," whatever that meant. And, in the back of my mind, all I could remember was my brother's words, telling me that I would tarnish our family's name.

I ended up graduating from Eastern Michigan University with a bachelors, masters, post-masters, and a 4.0 GPA. During my time there, I worked at the LGBTQIA+ resource center for three years, became the International Student Association president, and achieved the Outstanding Student of the Year Award for a tobacco-free policy I wrote for the student body that was approved by administration. All of this to say that I was dedicated to proving my brother wrong, and I did.

However, there was something still lacking. Moving to the US was a significant cultural shift, specifically in regards to my sexuality.

Dating in the US is not the same as Pakistan, that's for sure.

I started using dating apps, many of which are banned in Pakistan, to meet people. Wanting to be straightforward, I mentioned that I am a side in my bio, and I was instantly rejected with four simple words, "This ain't gonna work." This was weird to me because, while it was a more niche subset of the gay community, penetration had never seemed like such a big deal in Pakistan. Many gay men I knew were not open to penetration and relationships would work around it. It seemed like this component of sex was so central in the US gay culture that without it, relationships were moot.

Some guys that could get past the bio would text me for a few days, set up a date in a park or coffee shop somewhere, and then stand me up with no explanation. The first time I was stood up, I was so confused and surprised. From my experience, men in Pakistan don't ghost other men, let alone stand them up. They are much more straightforward about their interest because there is a great deal of concern for maintaining relationships and respect within the community. That level of consideration seemed to be lacking here and it became increasingly clear that the gay men I spoke with were only concerned for their individual happiness and comfort.

It almost seemed like the dating culture in the US was an open market where men would shop around, only looking out for themselves, tossing unwanted belongings into a pile on the floor for someone else to pick up. In my experience, men seem to be constantly searching for one perfect man who meets all of their requirements. They match, meet, and move on so quickly, that I don't know if they ever even find this perfect person. Because at the end of the day, people aren't perfect and we have to adjust to shortcomings and learn how to build the perfect love out of imperfect individuals.

Despite this being most of my new reality, I eventually met a guy that I really liked. We had very similar thoughts on life, love, and relationships, and we connected easily. However, after many romantic dates, including home-cooked meals, handmade cards, and a level of physical intimacy I was comfortable with, we hit a wall. In my culture, sons live with their parents in order to take care of them. I take care of the house, do their taxes, pay their car payments, and cover their health insurance. They are my dependents. Unfortunately, that seemed to be in contradiction with the men I met, who valued their independence from their parents and seemed to look down on me for having this "additional responsibility."

I remember breaking down in a meeting one day, exhausted with the number of unsuccessful "matches" I had had, craving some kind of sustainable and healthy partnership. My coworker immediately set me up with a counselor who could talk me through what I was going through. Straight allies are so much easier to come by here because, at a higher level, society can be so much more accepting. One thing I really appreciate about the US is that I automatically felt safer to be myself, loud and proud, because of the strong culture of independence.

I was a little hesitant about meeting with this counselor, though, because resources for gay people in Pakistan are not great, to say the least. A friend of mine came out to his therapist during a session and was then forced to watch female pornography and analyze nude photos to arouse himself into "correcting." Many therapists in Pakistan have also preached that you become what you think, so you are only gay if you think you're gay.

However, this counselor connected me with a Queer Muslim Group in the area and communities that would make me more comfortable with who I am. My counselor helped me cope with my worries about finding a partner and redirected my focus to be more confident in my identity as a side. I felt like I didn't have to hide myself and, while that made me happy, it made me sad for the LGBTQIA+ community in Pakistan, because I know that if they had resources like this, they would be so much stronger.

I am so incredibly proud of the queer community in Karachi. We have been through so much and have cultivated a support structure like no other. LGBTQIA+ nurses and doctors discreetly volunteer their time to offer free health care services to queer folks through an underground hospital. We form instantaneous bonds with people we barely know and jump at the chance to help them with whatever they need, simply for identifying as one of us. We are a community like no other.

And, I am also proud of the queer community in the US. While it is harder to develop deeper bonds, the grassroots efforts by these individuals has pushed institutions far beyond what I grew up knowing. From legal bills to access to PREP, the history and commitment to equality here was fought for and runs so deep within the fabric of this society.

There will always be good and bad things within different societies and part of immigrating means understanding the need to adapt. The social support that existed in Pakistan does not exist here, just like the open communities, support groups, and resources don't exist there. So, as I learn to make do in this new society, I need to dance between the good and bad in both cultures, holding onto what feeds me and letting go of what doesn't.

Contributor's Bio:

Mr. Patel (he/him) is a Clinical Research Coordinator at Michigan Medicine. He has over 3 years of experience as a data manager in gastrointestinal, soft tissue (sarcoma), and thoracic cancer clinical trials. He earned a graduate degree in Health Education and post-masters certificate in Good Clinical Practice (GCP) from Eastern Michigan University. He is actively involved in organizing the series of health awareness programs for college students. He also volunteers at local multicultural events as a singer and a Bollywood dancer to promote international diversity in Southeast Michigan.

The Gift

Kavi

Pooja Aunty called me fat one time. I was at their house for a playdate, and we'd all been rummaging around in her front yard, searching for bugs underneath rocks. I'd gone inside for a glass of water, and there was Pooja Aunty sorting through a stack of mail. She smiled at me as I walked in. "You girls are growing up so much now," she said, and I'd paid it no mind. Aunties loved to talk about how much you were growing up, and pinch your cheeks, and tell you how cute you were. They didn't always look you up and down, the way that Pooja Aunty was doing now, but it happened. "Especially you," she continued, "you're getting so big, Ketaki!" She didn't meet my eyes; instead, they fixated somewhere just below that. I looked down and saw my belly, saw the way that it poked out from my bright pink t-shirt, refusing to be contained by the polyester blend. Maybe she didn't actually say "fat," but aunties never use their words to tell you. I'd gotten the message—Your body is wrong. You need to start worrying about it.

If the shame felt at all escapable then, it quickly surrounded me as my mother joined in. "You're getting so big, Ketaki," my mother said with a laugh, poking at my belly. It was a few weeks after we'd gone to Pooja Aunty's. I laughed too. It was funny how much everyone cared about my stomach. The teasing continued, but sometimes there were comments, too. "Tishya's mom told me you ate four sandwiches at her place yesterday." I'd hesitate. Was that bad? Did I do something wrong? She'd never tell me. But I understood from the poke at my belly, the pinching of my arms. Soon, she was making sure I ran around at least five times a day, and that I signed up for gymnastic lessons, and that I wasn't eating anything in between meals. That I would never, ever, dare to ask for seconds.

My mother explained it all to me one morning on the way to school. I sat in the back seat of our Honda Pilot, playing with the strap of my backpack. Each poke at my belly, each rule, each admonition was a lesson, a labor of love. She was showing me that people would treat me better if I shaved my legs, hid my breasts, and kept my stomach as flat as could be. She had to learn the hard way, but she wanted me to realize it sooner. The culmination of all her experiences, the lessons learned - this was her gift to me. I couldn't see her face, but I saw her eyes as they met mine in the rearview mirror. I knew she was telling me the truth. I thought about how my friend Jaya said my stomach was as big as a watermelon. If I followed her rules, I wouldn't have to worry about that. Aunties wouldn't talk about me and embarrass my mother how she told me they did. All I had to do was accept her gift, and I would make our lives easier.

The aunties' stares, my mother's rules, and my friend's teasing—it all came in such quick succession, and suddenly I was so sure that I was wrong. Wrong for existing in the way that I was. Wrong for not changing myself more. Wrong for my stomach, for my hunger. A wrong body that needed to be changed. So, for a time, I listened to my mother and accepted her offering. I shaved my legs and underarms. I went with her to wax my eyebrows and upper lip. I wore shapewear and sweaters paired with matching earrings. Conformity was a grueling affair. It wasn't just the clothes or the sting of the wax strip as it left my underarm. There was the guilt about sneaking food out of the kitchen, the debasing step onto the bathroom scale, the dizziness of running for an hour and seeing how long you could go without eating after—the exhaustion of trying to make myself right. Perfection was the ultimate goal, and for the briefest moment, it seemed attainable. I didn't realize, though, that you could only follow the rules for so long. The desire starts to eat away at you, reminding you of all the things you can't have.
Cake. Candy. Crop tops. Women.

I came out to my mother my sophomore year of college, in the passenger seat of the Honda Pilot on the way home from dinner. The second the word bisexual left my lips, I knew I'd betrayed her. I'd given the world a weapon to wield against me, despite everything she'd taught me. I had thrown away the work she'd put into preventing the pain of being different. We drove around for hours that night, so she could tell me just how angry she was. I was too mean, too loud, too fat, and now too gay to be accepted. The admonitions grew, her rage persisted, and I started to cry—shakily, silently, so as not to interrupt her. When she turned to look at me, and our eyes met, I saw her pain. And suddenly, I couldn't stop seeing it - woven into her angry words, peeking through her shaking hands. Hidden in her gift.

I will not inherit my mother's trauma.

That's what I told myself after, as I started to push myself to wear what she told me I couldn't, to eat what she would hate me for eating. It was my mantra as I broke rule after rule in an effort to find myself. My legs got hairier, and my clothes got baggier, and my bra went unworn. I made gay friends, listened to gay songs, danced at gay clubs, and outed myself to anyone who would talk to me.

In between semesters, I went home to my mother and Pooja Aunty and all the other reminders that it was easier and better to be the person that fits in. My mom would book me appointments with the eyebrow lady and remind me to shave. She would make me change if we were going to visit someone. Aunties would tell me how much I'd grown, and sometimes there would be stares. But that was all—stares. I wondered why my mother cared so much about what they said to her. It strengthened my resolve to ignore what she'd tried to pass on to me.

Nine months after I came out to my mother, I tried on my first binder in the bathroom of the Multicultural Student Services Center with my two best friends. The Center had a free binder program, and we'd decided to take advantage. We each picked out a different color - mine was white - and decided we couldn't wait to try them on. The fabric was thick, like the shapewear that my mom would buy for me in middle school. As I pulled it on, the resemblance grew more unnerving. I looked at myself in the mirror, t-shirt and jeans with my binder underneath, and I didn't recognize myself. My t-shirt didn't stick out the way it usually did. I liked it. I kept it on the whole way back to my apartment and all the way through doing my homework. I took pictures. I wore it for a week straight after that, trying on old outfits and relishing the way they looked so much better when my chest was flat.

I didn't always hide my chest. Some days I'd wear my binder, and some days the sight of its constricting fabric made my lungs ache in remembrance. When my chest was bound, I could wear skirts that rode up to my thighs with bright t-shirts to match. On days where my body protested, I'd throw on my oversized orange trench coat or my too-big jean jacket and hope for the best. The binder did nothing to hide my stomach, which would still jut out, resolute in the face of any attempt at constriction. I got in the habit of looking down at it once I put my binder on. Patting at it, rubbing it. Hiding it under my high-waisted jeans.

Until then, the shame my mother had instilled about my breasts had felt unavoidable. I wondered if my excitement about binding came from the same part of me that hid my stomach and plucked my brows and dieted. The part that I was trying to disown. I wanted to know why I was binding my chest. I wanted to know that I was performing being transgender correctly. I wanted to know if I was doing it right or faking it for attention. And was I really bisexual, or was that yet another extension of my insecurities? Who would I be without that fear of being wrong? It still mattered to me what people thought of me. I didn't think anyone would see me as worthy of affection or respect if I didn't look a certain way. I thought of my mother's face the night I came out to her. She looked like I'd sentenced myself to be forever in pain. And I still didn't understand why.

It took some time for the understanding to happen, for the memories to collect into something coherent. My mother did her eyebrows before she went to the bank. She wore perfume the day we went to buy a new car, and she didn't say a word the entire time. She made me talk to the sales representative on the phone because he didn't understand her accent. She called my dad to make sense of the letter she got from the insurance company. My aai, my mother, did everything she could not to be seen as unfit in a world that was not built with her in mind. Conformity was the only viable means of escape. If she were thinner, flatter, prettier, nicer, maybe people wouldn't care so much about her accent. Aunties will forever complain, and, as it turns out, so will white America. The pain and fear she felt came because the wrongness would always exist, in some way or another—people would always find a reason to see it.

Growing up, it felt like everyone else had figured themselves out, and it was just me that was struggling. I admired the way my classmates were effortlessly beautiful in a way that I never was. To go from admiration to desire was intuitive. I inherited my mother's insecurity, and it lived in my sexuality. The grief she gave me about my body made me feel good about binding my chest, in hiding it like she wanted to. But it was her gift – the trauma of never, ever, meeting society's standards – that gave me the confidence to find myself. It let me discard the pretense of gender and all its hidden conformities. My mother's trauma doesn't just live within me; it sets me free.

Contributor's Bio:

Kavi (they/them) is a diaspora Indian, raised in a family defined by conformity to the rules. As a 21-year-old, queer, non-binary person, they still find themselves wrestling with hegemony. As a Buddhist, they have learned that through struggle comes ambiguity comes art. Kavi recently graduated from George Washington University with a BA in Political Science and is currently pursuing a Masters in Public Health in Health Promotion. Having worked in a variety of non-profit, activist, and educational spaces, they hope to give every person a fighting chance to help the world become a better, more accepting place.

Wrenched Apart

Nita Sen
as told to Editor

I skipped up the stairs of the Frank Porter Graham Student Union building and ducked into room 3102. It was a central space, and I worried about being spotted as I entered our LGBTQIA+ student organization's mass meeting. Neither my friends nor my family knew I was bisexual. With the large but surprisingly tight-knit, brown population on campus, I tried to be as discreet as possible. I could feel my heart beating fast, both from the fear of being caught and the anticipation of what this meeting might mean for me.

I pictured a new chapter of self-discovery. Coming to terms with my sexuality was a defining milestone, but building a community of queer folks where I could be myself would solidify my sense of identity and authenticity. I yearned to finally say the words out loud to someone that would understand the pain, guilt, happiness, and fulfillment that comes with them. I felt ostracized in so many brown communities because, between the heteronormativity and blatant homophobia, no one was out, and I wasn't ready to be the first one. I had spent most of the past year hiding behind my brownness, and I was ready to embrace this facet of my identity finally.

Peering into the room, I guiltily hoped not to encounter any South Asians that might recognize me. It wasn't like I didn't want brown people in this queer space, but the fear of being recognized and outed balled up in the pit of my stomach. Evident by my freezing fingers and sweaty palms, I was conflicted by this feeling. But when the heavy oak door cracked open, what I saw was shocking and disappointing. Growing up, it wasn't uncommon for me to be the only person of color in a room, but with the "welcoming to all" slogan attached to the flyer for this event, I expected more diversity. This meeting was meant to be a pre-Pride event, and my mind was overwhelmed with assumptions about what this meant Pride would look like. To me, it meant one of two things: either there weren't many people that look like me in the LGBTQIA+ community, or there were, but they chose not to be in spaces like this. I didn't know which was more worrisome.

As an introvert that had just spent forty-five minutes convincing myself to show up and "put myself out there," I knew I had to make the most of it. I folded away all feelings of discomfort and embarrassment and let my longing to feel included push me forward. I stood in a corner, attempting to hover near conversations, pretending to laugh here and there as a hopeful ice breaker. Although I came to this community looking for acceptance for my queer identity, all I felt was out of place in my queer *brownness.*

I made eye contact with a small group near the food table and tried to strike up a conversation. After awkward introductions, the discussion quickly transitioned into people sharing their coming out stories and experiences with dating apps on campus, and it was clear I couldn't relate. Although this was the first meeting of the semester, I already felt like I didn't belong. I did my best for a few more minutes and then admitted defeat.

During the 15 minute walk home, I went back and forth about going to the upcoming Pride event. For me, the purpose of this meeting was to make a group of friends to go to Pride with. I wanted solidarity and encouragement, but I left with loneliness. There were two voices in my head: one wanted me to be brave and embrace this part of myself even if that meant going alone; the other felt like a scared little kid lost in a casino, out of place and alone. In the end, I settled with half going. This essentially meant attending the event but standing on the outskirts.

The festival had shut down four interconnecting streets on the south side of campus to create an open quad area. The typically busy streets were taken over by taco stands, carnival food carts, giant posters, and booths with free giveaways. There was also a stage set up on the right-hand side for drag performances and singing and dancing competitions. When I entered the quad, people were getting ready to meander. I decided to arrive pretty early in the day to check things out before it got too crowded. I stood by some trees wrapped in fairy lights and streamers and focused intently on the coffee in my hand so I wouldn't look too awkward by myself.

There was music playing and people talking, and groups of attendees moving closer towards the stage. People laughed and danced around with friends, seemingly having a great time. I saw people with friends who loved and accepted them for being all of who they were, and I wished I had that. I saw people in matching t-shirts, and almost everyone came with a group of people, while I stood there, alone. The juxtaposition of their joy and my anxiety made me feel even more isolated. I also noticed that, again, I was one of few visibly presenting people of color, and the only South Asian person, at the event.

As tears of isolation and a lack of belonging began to well up in my eyes, I decided it was time to leave. I was disappointed in myself for feeling anxious and out of place. I knew why I was leaving, but there was still that voice in my head telling me to be brave and wanting me to see this through. Maybe if I stayed longer I would have seen more people of color or found a group of people, or perhaps even one person, to hang out with. But Pride events are supposed to focus on joy and celebration – literal pride. I didn't know if I had it in me to be proud when I was struggling to be comfortable as my whole self.

These two events felt so formative to my queer identity. They were the first queer spaces I allowed myself to enter. But, while these queer-focused events affirmed my queerness, I exited feeling isolated in my brownness. If it is this hard to find queer South Asian people in college, a place where people are typically more exploratory of their identities, what would this mean for finding my place in queer spaces after graduation? If all of me couldn't be present, how could I navigate the intersection of these identities?

Would I always feel like an outsider?

In another attempt to explore my bisexuality, I decided to try dating. I thought it might be an easier, low-stakes introduction to the queer community in Chapel Hill.

Unfortunately, I was wrong...

Phrases like, "I've always wanted to date a brown person" and "I heard brown girls are willing to try all kinds of things" pushed me out even more. One girl even asked me if I could wear a *bindi* while we had sex. The absence of South Asian representation in the LGBTQIA+ community created so many false biases and stereotypes about what it meant to be brown and queer that I felt exoticized, fetishized, objectified, tokenized. Any negative past participle, I felt it. Discouraged, I retreated from this identity again.

The following year, a friend introduced me to Aurora. She was quiet and shy at first, but as our daily texts turned into hour-long video chats, I discovered a spunky and confident side to her. I felt deeply connected to her early in our friendship and came out to her. It wasn't long before I realized I had feelings for her. She eventually asked me to be her girlfriend and, of course, I said yes. I grew to love her, but, most of all, I admired her. She had been out as gay since middle school and was an example of what it could be like to feel confident in one's identities. Our relationship seemed different because it blossomed out of a friendship that was nurtured and watered over time with love, trust, safety, and comfort. It felt natural and easy like she saw me for my truth instead of a collection of stereotypes. This was partly because she had had her own experiences navigating stereotypes and biases as a Jewish woman.

I became more comfortable in queer bars and at queer events throughout our relationship because she gave me the "small-scale community" I needed. While the racial makeup of these places did not change, I now had an in: my partner. I came to the sad realization that these are the limited spaces we have as queer people, and if I wanted to embrace my queerness, I had to separate it from my brownness.

This resignation created a more significant divide between my South Asian identity and my queer identity. It reinforced that South Asian people are not welcome in queer spaces and that queerness was not accepted by South Asian people. As a result, I internalized this and became increasingly, and disappointingly, comfortable keeping those identities separate.

My typical Friday night became dance practice with my Bollywood dance team, followed by drag night at our local gay bar. I made the conscious decision not to tell my dance team where I was going after practice, let alone introduce them to my girlfriend or other queer friends. This was my fourth semester on the team and, during this time, no one was out and everyone identified as cis-gendered. It is possible that queer people had been on the team in the past or were currently on the team, but the fact that no one boldly shared their LGBTQIA+ identity meant it was probably a risk I shouldn't take. Our practices were often littered with homophobic rhetoric when boys rolled their hips a certain way, strict gender roles in the way partners were assigned, and transphobic jokes when costumes were designed. But, I grew up in a traditional Bengali family and was socialized to believe this behavior was expected. I decided to let them know me as they currently knew me and not complicate the relationship.

Slowly, I started to come out to people individually—small-scale introductions. I came out to my best friend on the team and cried the whole time, mentally preparing for her to shut me down or question my authenticity. She was supportive, and I asked her to keep it a secret.

Then, I came out on *Facebook* by adding my girlfriend to my relationship status. Hey, it was 2011, and officially dating meant *Facebook Official*. I was so proud of myself for being brave, but I didn't want to be stupid. I restricted viewing access on the post for all my South Asian friends and family. It was ridiculous and exhausting to go through my friend list, sifting them out and making my best guess about who might not be "safe" to come out to. But, I worried about their judgment and disbelief. I wanted to protect both myself and Aurora. The last thing I wanted was for her to be on the receiving end of the homophobic comments that I had heard my friends and family members make about others in the past. So, I was half out of the closet...

Sometimes, though, Aurora and I would take weekend trips to cottage towns where neither of us would run into anyone we knew … and we actually held hands in public! This was terrifying but felt so fulfilling. The fear of what strangers might say or do at the sight of a same-gender, interracial couple was still present, but the freedom and authenticity I felt made it so worthwhile. So, we held onto and cherished each of those secret moments.

Although Aurora tried to understand my situation, the secrecy became challenging for both of us. My sister knew about our relationship, and my parents knew her as a friend. I wished we could exist more authentically and romantically in brown spaces, but I wasn't ready yet. While I wouldn't say that was the cause of our relationship ending, it was an added layer. We were both dealing with our own demons and eventually decided it'd be best for both of us to break up. Throughout our relationship, she helped me grow as a person and become more comfortable and open with my queerness. I will forever be grateful for her love, acceptance, and patience.

My next romantic relationship happened to be with a man. Externally, my bisexuality felt invisibilized by being in a deceptively "heterosexual" relationship. Internally, I held on to my blossoming confidence with my sexuality and myself.

After graduation, I grew exasperated with constantly hiding and separating the different parts of myself. When I moved to a new state to start graduate school, I decided to start fresh and be openly out to people in my program, which included South Asians. It was terrifying, but taking that first step felt rewarding. I received positive affirmation and acceptance from many and judgment and condescension from a select few. But none of that mattered. I could finally exist as my whole self, and I felt lighter.

From then on, I continued to seek representation of queer people of color to demolish the belief that being queer is a "white people thing." While there was definitely more representation in the media than when I was younger, it still felt removed from reality. There was little to no representation within my extended family and closer-knit Bengali community. I would spend evenings swiping through social media and blog pages searching for queer South Asian representation, and every time I stumbled upon a profile punctuated by a rainbow flag, I felt a little less alone.

Then one day, my mom sent me a screenshot of a family friend's daughter, who came out on *Facebook* as bisexual. The six words in the text message that followed radiated my heart like only a mother's embrace can:

"I'm really proud of this girl."

Seeing someone in our community be publicly proud was awe-inspiring. And my mom's positive response to the post gave me the confidence I needed to call my mom and come out to her. Initially, she laughed, assuming I was joking. I smiled back and explained the seriousness of it and why I kept it hidden for so long. I could relate my situation to the girl from the post, making it easier for my mom to process. The conversation had its challenges, but I slowly started to feel like my brownness and queerness could coexist within me.

I decided to pursue a career as a psychologist, specializing in polysexual identities and interracial or mixed-orientation relationships. I became more intentional about sharing my sexual orientation with others to become the representation that I lacked all my life. While working on a college campus, I co-founded a Queer and Trans People of Color organization as a support group for students with these identities. Every time we get together, it still surprises me the difference that this space makes for the young people I work with and myself. Even as I help others navigate this complicated identity, I am still on my journey of exploration to determine how to exist as both queer and brown proudly.

Finding a space where I feel comfortable living in this intersection is still challenging sometimes, and I don't believe that sentiment is unique to my journey. There are days I wake up and pour coffee into my Pride 2018 mug and feel irrevocably whole in my identities. There are also days I overhear homophobic microaggressions at the local Indian grocery store. As the shopkeeper winks at my husband and me, I realize he assumes I am straight. I toggle back and forth between these identities, struggling to pull both parts of me together. Hopefully, one day I'll get there, but for now, I still feel wrenched apart.

Contributor's Bio:

Nita Sen (she/her) is a bi/pansexual ciswoman in an interracial, intercultural, and interreligious relationship who has always felt like her various identities were never allowed to exist simultaneously. She is a therapist who seeks to provide others what she never got growing up.

India's Secret Obsession

Avery Wilde
as told to Editor

Sex is ubiquitous in Indian culture. People hint at sex in advertising, in movies, in music videos. I'm talking about Govinda and Karishma Kapoor dry humping in *Sarkai Liyo Khatiya*, or Kangana Ranaut laying shirtless on a man's bareback for a Levis ad, or literally any Katrina Kaif item number. Without ever explicitly saying it, sex is used everywhere, often by sexualizing women. But no one actually talks about sex or sexuality.

The India that I know has always had a conservative view on sex. Growing up, we were told by parents, *pandits*, and pedagogues that sex was an act practiced for the sake of having children and not to be discussed. Given our invention of the Kama Sutra and our 1.3 billion population, I can confidently say this iron fist approach to sex has been unsuccessful in limiting the sex that was clearly happening right under their noses.

However, what it did limit was our understanding of sex and sexuality. We never learned about consent, pleasure, pain, precautions, or birth control. There was no such thing as sexual education – not heterosexual sex ed and definitely not queer sex ed. Was the lack of discussion supposed to act as a form of control? As though not acknowledging queer sex or any kind of sex would prevent it from happening? Regardless, we took it upon ourselves to learn from the 3 F's: films, friends, and the fucking internet.

It was during a random internet search when I stumbled upon Section 377. I learned that queer sex, and thus queerness, was illegal. It was lumped alongside sex with animals and was punishable by life imprisonment. It didn't make sense to me. As a country, we refuse to acknowledge or discuss sex. We pretend like it doesn't happen. Until it comes to controlling who people can and can not have sex with. When same-sex partners engage in consensual sex, we ring the bells and blow the whistles, and if the culprits are lucky, they live long enough to spend the rest of their days in jail.

To be honest, I was pretty removed from this law and its implications at the time because I identified as straight. As selfish as it sounds, the law didn't affect me, so I didn't think much of it. This was until talk of queerness and sexuality penetrated my friend circles. I don't know how, but almost overnight, friends started attending and organizing protests and criticizing Bollywood's comedic and satanic depiction of homosexuality. I began realizing that I didn't know too many people who were queer in India, at least none that were out. Until that point, the only time I engaged with people who would fit on the LGBTQIA+ spectrum was meeting people who identified as third gender at family weddings and functions.

They are often referred to by many derogatory terms across India, but are formally recognized as the third gender in India, neither man nor woman. There is no direct translation for their gender or sexual identity in Western terms. They are seen as the purest people in the world, so they are often invited to bless big functions. During these blessings, the reactions they typically receive are, "Just hand them this money and ask them to leave." Outside of these events, they are completely rejected by society and left to fend for themselves, scrambling to acquire low-paying jobs and facing regular violence by the state and police.

Once, I was sitting in our car, baking in the pre-monsoon heat, while my mom went to a nearby dress shop to pick up an order. The roads were busy, and I fixed my eyes on the radio station so I wouldn't catch anyone's attention. There was a light tap on my window, and I looked up, expecting my mom to be retrieving a forgotten purse. I never asked for her name, but she was part of the third gender community and was smiling down at me, asking for money. I searched my pockets and the cupholder where we typically store loose change and couldn't find anything. I turned to the woman and apologetically shook my head. She said it was okay and wished me well with eyes so soft and kind that I'll never forget them.

When my mom got back into the car, I asked her why the only time we see people from the third gender community is when they are begging for money. She explained the discrimination they face in India without ever directly calling it discrimination. She said while the law and historical Indian culture acknowledges their gender, society will never accept them because they are "different." Employers are worried they will ruin their companies' reputation, so no one offers them jobs. They don't have a choice other than begging to survive. Society marginalized them in an effort to silence their community's voice, as if pretending like they don't exist would cease them from existence.

I nodded pensively, reflecting on the stories I had learned about in Hindu scripture. The *Rigveda*, an ancient collection of Sanskrit hymns, talks about life beyond a gender binary. In the *Ramayana*, Hanuman describes *rakshasa* women, demonesses, kissing and embracing other women. The walls of *Kharjuraho* temple, a World Heritage Site, are covered with carvings of women intimately embracing one another. There are many examples beyond these that depict fluidity in gender and sexuality. So, where does it all go wrong? Why do we pretend this doesn't exist?

Excerpts of religion point one way, but law and society point the other. For a government that prioritizes Hinduism above other religions, our laws and culture directly contradict religious canon. God preaches forgiveness and acceptance, but we condemn and vilify. And if that doesn't work, we shame into silence.

The more I thought about the intricacies of sexuality within our conservative culture, the more involved I became as an ally, and the more I began to discover my own sexuality. I was terrified, to say the least. The toughest part was, while there was some accessible information about being gay or lesbian if you searched hard enough, there was almost nothing about being bisexual. I had no idea how to proceed, where to turn for help, or what having sex with a woman would even look or feel like.

My plan was simple. I would be leaving for university in Australia in a few weeks, and I would come out shortly before that. I was terrified of telling people other than my trusted friends at this point. News spreads like wildfire in our community, and a tiny flame could ignite my life. However, when my parents mentioned arranging my marriage, I realized I had to tell them soon before they heard it from someone else.

One day, a Panditji, a priest, showed up at my house, and, overcome by a fever of fear that resulted from holding this secret in for too long, I assumed he was there to "fix me" for being queer. In actuality, the Panditji came to ask for donations, but that fear pushed me to unburden myself of the pressure that had been festering within me. Unfortunately, after coming out to my parents, I did not receive the open arms and acceptance I yearned for. They made assumptions that this meant I just wanted to have sex with everyone and recommended I keep it to myself to protect my reputation and job prospects. Since then, they have made it clear that they will never accept my sexuality.

Suffice it to say, I was ready to leave.

It wasn't easy to transition from a country where sex was virtually a forbidden topic of discussion to a place where sex seemed like a word casually tossed into common conversation. Over time, I made friends and found a community that pushed me to be myself, in whatever form that took. I was liberated to explore my sexuality among people who didn't care if I was gay or straight. Although gay marriage wasn't legal yet, the Australian society offered me the freedom to meet people, the encouragement to advocate for my rights without fear of backlash, and the resources to understand what gender, sexuality, and sex actually meant for me. I never felt more like myself.

I know this seems typical; an Indian studying in the west idealizing this new, western culture. I guess the "idealism" came from the fact that I needed to get outside of my culture to understand the shackles it placed on my relationship with my sexuality, and when I did, I realized I didn't want to return to those shackles. To be clear, I love India. I just wish it loved me enough to free me from its "*chup-chup*" ("don't talk about it") approach to sex and sexuality.

During those 30 minute calls with my parents every other day, I had to readjust my tone, openness, and opinions to be their "perfect, conservative Indian daughter." I don't believe this was entirely falsified, but I also knew that I couldn't fully be myself. While my sister did her best to slowly introduce them to queer shows and issues in an effort to make my sexuality more comprehensible to them, the illegality and unfamiliarity of the concept made it, in their words, "gross."

Over time, though my sister and I attempted to plant seeds, typically articles and memes via WhatsApp, they did not budge in their belief and maintained that I keep this private. This made it clear to me that India at large wasn't ready for this fully liberated view on sex and sexuality. The conservatism that plagues India has borne sour fruit from these rotten roots. This fruit has come in the form of homophobic elected officials, business leaders that speak down on the queer Indian community, and colonies of aunties sharing spicy gossip over hot pakoras and chai. And these fruits sprinkle their seeds over the rest of society, spreading their harmful thinking to individuals like my parents.

On September 6th, 2018, the Indian court ruled unanimously in Navtej Singh Johar v. Union of India that Section 377 was unconstitutional. I heard stories about celebrations in the streets, underground communities that came to the surface, and couples that went to police stations to request impromptu weddings. Unfortunately, all that was legalized was sex, and their requests were promptly denied, give or take a few rude comments and snickers, hidden behind tobacco stenched breaths.

You see, changing the law was a giant wave that accomplished only a ripple of progress because it focused solely on the act of sex. There was no discussion about destigmatizing sex or sexuality, no guidelines of what constituted discrimination against LGBTQIA+ people, and no education about the LGBTQIA+ experience for the larger society. Some of these issues have been addressed by social media and local nonprofits, but in the small town I am from, little has improved in terms of mentality. We still don't talk about sex or sexuality.

And how can I expect my parents to embrace me in the fullness of my sexuality if they don't hear about others like myself, if they don't know we exist in commonplace? If they were raised to avoid discussing distasteful topics like sex? Obviously, I can't expect them to fathom discussing sexuality.

We need sex education that is inclusive of all sexualities and genders, not just to support those vulnerable in society but also to change the minds of those in power. We need politicians to come forward in support of the repeal of Section 377. We need to encourage conversations that normalize sex and sexuality. While I was afforded the privilege to study in a country where I experienced the freedom to define sex and sexuality for myself, the answer to our society's progress is not for our people to leave the country. The answer is to push our country to be better; isn't that patriotism?

I have been overwhelmed and inspired by the local community organizers across the country doing this work. The Pride marches that once happened in secret, dubbed "The Friendship Walk," now burst with color and vibrancy. Activists and legislators have received a glint of a spotlight on their grassroots efforts to advocate for better laws, more sex education, and additional support for the LGBTQIA+ community. Even the film industry has seen waves, including the recently released Made in Heaven, sharing the tale of a wedding planning agency in Delhi and starring a gay lead character. Society might not be ready, but the people are.

Section 377 being repealed should be a step towards having an open conversation about sex and sexuality because, without this, progress is impossible. Right now, the country's obsession with conservatism forces more people into hiding, which is not the mark of a developed society. I hope that we get to a point where I can say the word "sex" or "sexuality" and not receive a "*chi*" ("ew") in response. I hope we can talk openly and honestly about what sex looks like, feels like, and how to engage in it safely. I hope Indian society, and my parents, can come to accept sexual freedom like they do sexual connotations in all forms of media. It doesn't make me dirty or easy or "not family-friendly." It just makes me human.

Contributor's Bio:

Avery Wilde (they/them) was born and raised in India and moved to Australia for studies after turning 18. They have been there ever since, and they are incredibly grateful for the opportunity to build a life they can call their own. This story is about their life after realizing and accepting that they are bisexual. They have a blog on WordPress that they try to update when they can and an *Instagram* account they update every day. They also have friends and family who have been incredibly supportive.

All Roads Lead to Slash
Content warning: mentions of rape, death, and violence
Fatema Haque

Growing up, my physical world was compact. I woke up in the bedroom I shared with my dad and brother, walked two blocks to school, and returned home at 3 p.m. Once or twice a week, I walked to the library, which added another block to my commute.

When I started high school, my world expanded by 4.5 miles, and I got a room of my own. My commute now included a carpool service operated by a Bangladeshi *Chachi* (aunt-in-law). Every day, she drove nine other girls and me to school in her seven-passenger minivan, picking us up directly after school. This schedule left no room for me to participate in typical afterschool activities.

My conservative Muslim family and community further shrunk my physical world to the confines of our house. Girls weren't supposed to ride bikes, "roam around" the neighborhood, or sit on porches, lest we draw unwanted attention and gain a bad reputation. Looking outside at the tree-lined street, densely packed with single-family houses, only young boys could be seen skating on rollerblades, playing basketball, or doing wheelies on their bikes. Older men sat on porches, smoking, and chatting. Girls like me stayed indoors and occupied our time with studying, cooking, cleaning, or watching TV. Our social life happened over the phone, through backyard fences, or on occasional strolls in the alley behind our houses, away from the gossipy gaze of Bangladeshi neighbors.

It was this isolated existence that led me to watch soap operas, which had no seasons or summer hiatuses, and aired new episodes all year long. Finding the *General Hospital* fandom, an online community of fans, expanded that universe to unpredictable proportions.

I was twelve when I stumbled onto fandoms. In my seventh-grade computer class, I searched the web for Sonny Corinthos and Carly Benson, my favorite pairing on *General Hospital*. I expected to find spoilers and scanned images from *Soap Opera Digest*, issues of which I couldn't afford but read while trailing my family through the aisles of Kmart. I found these images on fan sites alongside hundreds of vignettes, short stories, and novels featuring Sonny and Carly; what I quickly learned was fanfiction* or fanfic. Fans of the show had written their own fictional versions of Sonny and Carly in the form of episode rewrites, missing scenes, and fix-it stories that transformed and added to the canon. They wrote alternate realities and explored Sonny and Carly's relationship through romance tropes such as love at first sight and fake dating. I had access to hundreds of new narratives for my favorite pairing with a single web search.

Not long after joining the *General Hospital* fandom, I learned of slash*, fanwork centered on the romantic and/or sexual relationship between characters of the same sex or gender. At first, slash existed only in the periphery of my fannish interests. In discussion boards, *AIM*, and *Yahoo! Groups* where fans like myself shared theories and analyses of characters, themes, and story arcs, someone would make the occasional homophobic joke about a romantic relationship between Sonny Corinthos and Jason Morgan, *General Hospital's* iconic mob boss/hitman duo. These "jokes" were frequently laced with misogyny, justifying Sonny and Jason setting off into the sunset with each other because the women in their lives were too "crazy," "dramatic," or "needy" to live with.

I recall participating in such "humor." Two men loving each other because they could and not because they couldn't make it work with the women in their lives was not yet within my capacity to imagine. I didn't know that queerness could exist independently and not as a response to failed heterosexuality. Time in fandom would teach me otherwise, however, since it had a long history of embracing queerness, with the first documented slash fanfics going back to the 1960s when *Star Trek: The Original Series* fans wrote and circulated Captain Kirk and Spock fanfic via private mail and in person at fan conventions.

My appetite for fanfic grew exponentially. To keep it satiated, my fannish interests swelled to include primetime fandoms: *Smallville*, *Everwood*, and *The O.C.*, among others. Fans of these shows seemed of a different caliber; the quality of art, writing, and meta-discussions was unlike anything I experienced in the *General Hospital* fandom. In these new fandoms, I saw fans consume and celebrate slash content at a rate that far outpaced heterosexual content. Slash was so popular that in a 2020 data analysis of the top 100 popular pairings on the Archive of Our Own (AO3), a non-commercial nonprofit archive of fanworks, slash pairings accounted for 1.2 million fanworks and made up 71 of the 100 most popular pairings.

Despite the increasing popularity of slash, I initially refrained from reading it because

I believed that I would not enjoy such stories and could not see the chemistry between same-gender characters that others saw. This belief began to change as more people within my fandom circles began writing and openly discussing slash works. In the early 2000s, slash fanworks grew exponentially because LGBTQIA+ rights gained increasing public support. On mainstream TV shows, such as *Dawson's Creek* and *All My Children*, queer characters were introduced, and other shows such as *Will and Grace* offered sanitized versions of queer lives. This public acceptance signaled a new era of tolerance. Previously, slash writers had experienced retaliation for sharing their works, with some being doxxed and outed at their places of employment and subsequently fired. Others were threatened or actively discouraged from sharing their works. With these fears of reprisals diminishing, slash writers felt safe enough to bring their works out of the trusted circles of private email lists and FTP archives into public discussion boards, blogging platforms, and web archives like Fanfiction.net where I repeatedly encountered them without having to actively seek them out.

Reading slash dramatically shifted my worldview: in slash fanfics, *Smallville's* Clark Kent and Lex Luthor were archnemeses and lovers instead of straight friends in a *bromance*, and Ryan Atwood was more attracted to Seth Cohen than the canonic heterosexual attachments on *The O.C.* These new narratives taught me how to queer media, that is, see the possibility of sexual and romantic attachment between characters irrespective of gender and canonic sexual identity.

By eleventh grade, queer relationships were so normalized and attractive to me that I began writing slash. Like most things in fandom, I learned by observing others. Fanfic had a standard format that included ratings, word counts, disclaimers to The Powers That Be to not sue the writer, and content warnings. Often, I saw writers put "slash" in the warnings, so I didn't think twice about doing the same, at least not until a fan questioned the practice. What about queer content elevated it to the level of rape, major character death, or graphic depictions of violence, they asked. Were readers ever warned about heterosexual content? (Spoiler alert: they weren't.) The subsequent dialogue on *LiveJournal*, a blogging platform and then-fandom hub, named the implicit heterosexism of the formatting convention.

These meta* conversations left indelible marks on me. Perhaps it was because the people participating in these conversations were my friends and mentors--people who exemplified the sort of creative, vulnerable, and supportive community that I didn't otherwise have access to. We were deeply involved in each other's lives. We faithfully read and commented on each other's blogs, celebrated birthdays and holidays with digital and physical gifts, and showed up for each other in times of crisis. I kept very little from them, talking frankly about my life. For a teenager spending all her time alone at home or at school, to feel so seen, heard, and accepted was everything. When I was struggling in calculus, a fandom friend connected me to another fan, an MIT graduate and NASA scientist, who tutored me over *AIM* for weeks until I could grasp the basics of limits and derivatives. Another friend helped me navigate conversations with my dad when I wanted to move away for college, something only one other person in my Bangladeshi community had done. When I struggled to pay for textbooks in college, fandom friends mailed me their copies. These people were there for me, and I trusted their advice and collective wisdom on all manners of things. Our relationship made it easy for me to listen, learn, and change my behavior. I went back to my slash fanfics and removed the warnings.

Years later, I was browsing the stacks of the University of Michigan Graduate Library when I recalled the Livejournal dialogue about slash in fanfic warnings and the fan who advocated for change. The memory surfaced unbidden as I searched for a memoir on growing up transgender and found it wedged between books about sexual predators and criminals. Furious and bewildered, I emailed a librarian. Why were books about transfolks lumped together with pedophiles and rapists, I asked, in much the same way the fan had asked why queer content was equated with rape and violence. I wondered what my then-partner, a transman, would have felt if he'd been the one to see books about transpeople shelved alongside "personality disorders, behavior problems including sexual problems, drug abuse, suicide, and child abuse." The librarian explained that those 60 odd books were published in the 1960s and 1970s when the Library of Congress grouped transsexualism with personality disorders and recatalogued them to "sexual life," where more modern texts on transgender lives were shelved. Without consciously realizing it, fandom had shown me how to fight for change.

Between 2002 to 2012, when fanfic saw increasing mainstream attention, it garnered harsh criticism and was labeled as "either porn, plagiarism, or otherwise creepy and gross."[1] It was sensationalized for poorly written erotica, rampant slashing as if that were a grotesque crime, and real person fiction, fanfic centering actual people rather than fictional characters. Often led by outsiders, these mainstream conversations missed the true purpose and exceptional power of fanfic.

Fanfic is an accessible form of creative expression, freely produced and consumed. Unlike other publication outlets, fanfic has low barriers to entry. Even someone like me, a homebound twelve-year-old with zero connections to a writing network, could publish her imaginings, instantly gain readership, and sustain the practice through an affirming community that gave her positive feedback and necessary mentorship.

Fanfic also afforded fans like myself the ability to write our truths into mainstream narratives that either erase or refuse to acknowledge us. Through narratives that capture our deepest desires for (queer) love, affection, comfort, and care, fanfic cultivates the readers' self-awareness and encourages community-building. During my first five years in fandom, I learned that being queer was normal and desirable, something to celebrate and support. I internalized this message, so much so that when I recognized my feelings for a same-gender friend as more than platonic, I felt secure. There were no doubts about myself; I didn't wonder if I was wrong or evil if I should force myself to be something other than what I was. Nothing in my physical world could've given me such confidence, but my experience in fandom and with slash taught me that all was okay. *I* was okay.

1. Romano, Aja. "The crumbling of the fourth wall: Why fandom shouldn't hide anymore." Daily Dot. 2 March 2020. https://www. dailydot.com/unclick/crumbling-fourth-while-fandom-shouldnt-hide/

In college, my fannish interest zeroed in on *Stargate: Atlantis (SGA)*, with the fan-favorite McShep (a portmanteau for Rodney McKay and John Sheppard) capturing my imagination. McShep fans were prolific, producing nearly 12,000 stories that keep McShep on the AO3 top 100 pairing list even today, eleven years after the last episode of SGA aired. The stories ran the gamut of romance tropes, covering everything from having to share a bed because it's the only option to finding intimacy by providing comfort to a character who has experienced physical pain or emotional distress. Of these tropes, my favorite was genderfuck, stories that explored gender, sexism, misogyny, and sexuality.

Genderfuck fanfics challenged my narrowly defined notions of masculinity. My physical reality was made up of Bangladeshi father figures who were breadwinners and wardens; boys who had all the freedom and none of the housekeeping responsibilities, as entitled and dependent on women's unacknowledged labor as their fathers. This aggravating reality wasn't exactly represented in mainstream media, which featured an endless lineup of white men and their version of patriarchy: guys like Clark Kent and Ryan Atwood were brawny and tough; boys like Seth Cohen and Ephram Brown were scrawny geeks, and men like Rodney McKay were middle-aged blowhards. With the exception of *Smallville's* Lex's affinity for the color purple, canonically straight, white, cis-men didn't deviate much from the confines of patriarchal masculinity.

In fanfic, though, patriarchal masculinity was repeatedly challenged. Fanfics where men were trapped in women's bodies by some magic or technology highlighted sexism, double standards, and misogyny. In *Ardhanarishvara* by Auburn and Monanotlisa, a McShep genderfuck epic weighing in at 425 pages, McShep, and co. agree to undergo gender reassignment for six months to acquire a planetary defense shield they encounter on a technologically advanced planet where citizens practice compulsory gender transition to keep the shield operational. Due to a genetic alteration, Rodney is unable to undergo the transition. John, on the other hand, does transition and then struggles with commanding a military base in a female body. He is further disturbed by Rodney's sexist treatment and his insistence on reversing their long-established protector/protected roles. None of this was radical in and of itself, as I was hyper-aware of living in a gendered world; however, the premise of compulsory transitioning flipped the script on our society's insistence on maintaining gender assigned at birth underscored the systemic oppression femme bodies face. Perhaps the most radical part of *Ardhanarishvara* is what happens after John transitions back to his male body: In a brief sequel, *The Red Dress*, we find that John's masculinity has broadened to include the feminine. He prepares his male body the way he did his female one, shaving all body hair, wearing a slinky red dress he had acquired months prior, and engaging in penetrative sex, something he didn't feel as enthusiastic about in his male body and masculine presentation.

Other fandoms further normalized gender nonconformity. In *Smallville* fanfics, Lex was often written as genderfluid, wearing makeup; in *Supernatural*, Dean Winchester's penchant for wearing women's lingerie was a launching point for negotiating his hypermasculine upbringing with his queer identity. Fanfic provided these genderfluid and gender-nonconforming narratives long before trans and nonbinary folks filled social media feeds, before characters like Eric Effiong on *Sex Education* stole our hearts, and before vocabulary such as nonbinary, genderqueer, femme, and genderfluid entered the vernacular. Consuming these works gently nudged me to understand and embrace nonrestrictive gender constructs, normalizing and broadening my c onception of queerness.

Despite generating radical transformative works, fandoms are not entirely immune to the shortcomings of their source materials. Fandoms can and will often mirror the racial and gender underrepresentation and erasure found across books, shows, movies, and other original works. For example, 68 of the 71 slash pairings in the AO3 top 100 are male/male, and of the 200 characters listed, only 52 are BIPOC. This disparity can be attributed to white male characters receiving the lion's share of screen time and being more fully developed than women, gender nonconforming, or BIPOC folks. Fandoms are built around attachment to characters. Fans who see potential in characters and feel a sense of connection with them through repeated, meaningful exposure then go on to produce fanworks. When the vast majority of these characters are white, cis-men, the fannish imagination is clipped before it can take off.

Nowhere is the impact of underrepresentation more apparent than in an author's note on a *Barsaat* (2005) fanfic I tried to write in 2009: "I'm only vaguely happy with [this fanfic] since I honestly don't know how femslash would work *in a Bollywood setting*." This note suggests that I observed enough chemistry between Anna Virvani and Kajal Kapoor, the two female leads in *Barsaat*, to attempt the story, and that femslash was in my wheelhouse, something I read and wrote. But it was not something I could imagine *in a Bollywood setting*, meaning between South Asian women. Looking back at this, I am disconcerted. Despite being a queer South Asian woman, despite spending a decade in fandom consuming queer literature, I couldn't see others like myself in their fullness, the way I could white characters. I couldn't imagine queerness existing within a South Asian identity. It seemed to me that a community that broadened my universe had reached its limits. It couldn't help me feel seen or make sense of my racial and cultural identities.

In May of 2009, I moved back to Bangladesh with the hope of reconnecting to my homeland. In the years that followed, I gradually withdrew from fandoms, shifting focus to my nascent career as an educator. I joined new physical communities and started learning about race and class. Black and Brown authors like bell hooks, Gloria Anzaldúa, Alice Walker, Audre Lorde, and Roxane Gay showed me how BIPOC women like myself could fully and vibrantly exist in literature. They wrote at the intersection of race, class, gender, and sexuality, which was everything I was grappling with, and their words helped fill the gaps that fandoms couldn't.

During my hiatus from fandoms, I constantly found myself reaching for the lessons I learned there. Fandoms taught me how to care for people and build community.

They taught me to listen and honor people's truths; to show up consistently; to provide emotional support when needed; to affirm people freely and often, without conditions or judgments; and when conflict arose--and it always did--to engage in dialogue, not censure. It taught me how to imagine new possibilities and keep an open mind. If something didn't jive well with me, it didn't make that thing wrong or bad; it didn't even mean that feelings of discomfort would be permanent. I felt uncomfortable with slash until I didn't. New things are like that; they can make us weary until we see enough of it until it becomes normalized, and I learned that in fandom better than anywhere else.

I returned to fandoms in 2018 after nearly a decade away. I reread fanfic I'd read as a teenager and felt the sort of comfort, solace, and joy that comes with revisiting old, familiar, well-loved things. I'm more cognizant than ever before of the representation issues in fandoms, but I also feel immense hope now that we have unprecedented access to diverse source content. What's most hopeful are the dialogues I'm witnessing in fandoms, ones that grapple with questions of representation, erasure, and justice, all while generating fanworks that make me think deeply about the world every day.

Contributor's Bio:

Fatema Haque (she/her) is a Bangladeshi American writer, educator, and community organizer based in Michigan. As a writer, she explores themes of love, healing, and self- / community-recovery. She's curious about ideas of home, family, and community; she often wonders what the world would look like if we lived into our truths, if we allowed our authentic selves a greater measure of freedom, if we loved women and other folks with marginalized identities more. Her writing can be found on her blog, fatemawrites.com.

Weirdness Points

Sensa
as told to Editor

When I was younger, I was introduced to the idea of "weirdness points." Essentially, a person has a limited number of points to spend on being different or unusual. There is no specific threshold, but you can tell when you are nearing your max by the ogling eyes and hushed whispers from aunties at dinner parties. "Weirdness points" is a term that I have found resonates with many queer people who have had to work through being the "different" one in their family or friend groups. This concept also translates into the context of South Asian families.

I visualize South Asian families as a web, where the more strongly connected the different strings are, the more tight-knit the web is. South Asian culture wants the web to be as tight-knit as possible, so you can't just cut one string between you and another person without the entire web collapsing. In contexts like this, you have to hold onto your weirdness points and spend them sparingly to preserve relationships.

As a child, while the other South Asian kids in my community clustered around singing and dancing and Bollywood, I was drawn to subcultures and countercultures. I became friends with the theater kids and "nerds," and I was excluded from most South Asian friend groups and community spaces. Weirdness points spent (-1). While I found like-minded people, I became very aware that I was the only South Asian in those spaces. I was often afraid to try out for lead roles in theater productions because the characters weren't written to be performed by brown people, and most other actors were white. I could never fully engage in cosplay with my friends because my skin color prevented me from authentically feeling like the predominantly white characters. I spent these weirdness points by letting my ethnicity "other" me into limiting my involvement (-2).

When I got to college, I decided I wanted to major in psychology—weirdness points spent (-3). My family didn't have a clear understanding of what I would do with a psychology degree and assumed I would go into Human Resources. When I told them I wanted to be a therapist, they were confused. As most brown uncles and aunties do, my extended family wrote therapy off as a "white people thing." They explained that white people don't talk to their families, so they spoke to therapists, but brown people didn't need therapy because they spoke to their families. Besides discouraging my career ambitions, this was hurtful because there were many things I felt like I couldn't talk to my family about.

Coming to terms with my pansexuality (-4) and gender fluidity (-5) during that time made me feel like I had beyond maxed out my allocation of weirdness points. My pansexuality never really felt like a massive revelation. It just felt like the default. Not being pansexual was like a fish grappling with the notion of not being in water. It just didn't make sense. Gender, on the other hand, still feels weird to me to this day.

Growing up, I would sometimes wish that I was a boy. I thought it was normal for girls, maybe as a coping mechanism for struggling against oppression as a gender minority. In a reading for one of my psychology classes, the concept was defined as penis envy. It felt like such a clear explanation of the dysphoria I experienced all my life, and I was so happy to finally have the verbiage for it. In class the next day, we discussed the reading, and the professor quickly called the concept out as "bullshit," explaining that women don't feel this way. That was when I realized that this feeling might not be "normal."

I still don't know if gender fluid is the exact term to use, but so far, it has seemed like the closest thing that fits. When I first started exploring what gender meant to me, I used a mood tracker app to record how femme or masc I felt each day. Some days, I would want to wear a dress and put on make-up, and others, the thought of the curves of my breasts and hips being visible through a t-shirt made me uncomfortable.

Although, it isn't just about expression through clothing –it is much deeper. It impacts the way I show up in the bedroom. Some days, when I am feeling more masculine, the last thing I want is to draw attention to my vagina when I am in bed with my partner. It impacts the pronouns I feel comfortable using. The first time I met someone that used they/them pronouns when referring to people whose pronouns had not been specified, I felt fireworks in my heart when they used "them" for me.

It's hard to explain exactly what gender feels like or when it feels right, but I know for a fact that picking between male and female just does not, and will not, make sense to me.

While my pansexuality felt normal, and gender fluidity was something I was still working through, I was intrigued by the idea of polyamory—weirdness points spent (-6). After college, I found my way to the kink community, which led me to the polyamory community. By this point, I didn't feel like I had any more weirdness points to spend and decided to invest in my own happiness instead. I attended a "Kinky Queer" event at a gay bar in San Jose and realized that people in the kink community* enjoyed dating multiple people so they could meet many kink needs. I remember having crushes on multiple people as early as middle school. I figured everyone did and just picked their favorite one to talk about at recess. Through many monogamous relationships, my partners and I were always open about discussing other people we had crushes on. I guess I just lucked out into dating partners who were pretty open.

I met my husband through the poly community. He and his ex were polyamorous because they were in a long-distance relationship, and a few months after they broke up, we started dating and later had a love marriage. This means our marriage was initiated by us, not arranged by family. Weirdness points spent, according to my traditional Indian family (-7).

Polyamory worked for us throughout our whole relationship. It gave me the opportunity to date women, something I ordinarily wouldn't be able to do because of family pressure, under the guise of a stable relationship with a cis-man.

Our relationship worked well for over five years. Eventually, we decided to get divorced—weirdness points spent (-8). The toughest part about the divorce was having to tell my family. I already couldn't afford to spend weirdness points when I got into this relationship, and now it seemed like I had to spend more to move on from it. I didn't care in the way I did when I was younger, but I knew it would be hard for my family because of the attention it would draw. The divorce was interesting, though, because we are still really good friends and continue to be in each other's lives. This ambiguity, once again, falls out of the norm of typical South Asian families. From experience, my family looks to blame someone for relationships that do not end well, and I worried that they might still blame him.

Eventually, I had to tell my mom about the divorce. She insisted on telling the extended family herself but kept coming up with excuses to delay sharing the news. First, she said she wanted to wait to see if it was real. Then, she used the pandemic as an excuse. Finally, she hit me with the big one; grandma's heart wouldn't be able to handle it.

Honestly, it made sense for her to tell them, and I trusted her to make the best decision. I always felt very distinct and different around my Indian family. Whenever I went home to visit, I constantly felt under inspection for everything from my mannerisms to my "Americanness."

It wasn't until I met a distantly related Aunty, who also happened to be a therapist, that I felt a little more "normal," like I belonged. When I walked through her front door the first time I met her, she received me with a long and warm embrace. The tightness with which she held me felt like it erased all the weirdness points I had ever spent (0). There was a sense of gratefulness and pride in her eyes that I had never seen in other elders before. As she relayed her experience working with substance abuse patients to me, there was an implicit "I'm so sorry you're going through so much" within each story. Over the last forty years, she had experienced what it felt like to challenge the norm, spend all your weirdness points in the hopes of helping others and understanding yourself, and still not be accepted. Since that meeting, I noticed a change in the way Aunties and Uncles responded to my job title. Now, I got a "You're helping people, and that's important."

In social policy, we are taught that things often start as unthinkable, then move to radical, acceptable, sensible, popular, and, finally, policy. To be honest, I always felt like my extended family was a step behind the social norm in these situations. My aunt entered this profession at the "unthinkable" stage, and I can not even imagine the hardship she faced. For me, being a therapist felt radical and shifted into becoming acceptable. Hopefully, it will become a respected profession in both my family and in the broader South Asian community with time.

This process of understanding where my parents' biases around sexuality, gender, and careers come from while balancing the differing perspectives from the multiple worlds I am part of has helped me become the therapist I am today. By unlocking the parts of myself that don't fit in with the cishet person I was supposed to be, I have unleashed a surplus of hope for the South Asian community. I know we can be better, and I hope that soon these weirdness points will become meaningless and our web will become tighter, but this time in a connection driven by love rather than preservation. At this moment, my bank of weirdness points are back to zero, but my heart and soul feel so full.

Contributor's Bio:

Sensa (they/them) is a Goan-American therapist, born/raised/living in the SF Bay Area. They have been fascinated by subcultures and intersectionality from a young age, and have made a career out of helping people navigate their socio-cultural landscape, processing unhealthy learned assumptions and behaviors, and creating the kind of support system and environment that they want. They are pansexual, polyamorous, and genderfluid, among other things.

part 4:

to the me i have become

Not The Beta You Thought You Knew
Not The Son You Thought You Knew

Adan Hussain

as told to Editor

Papa drank often and, when he did, our home was a challenging place to be. He had a short fuse while sober, but, when he was drunk, anything could set him off to be emotionally and sometimes physically abusive. I grew up in Queens, New York, as the only son of Pakistani Muslim immigrant parents. I observed the challenges Papa experienced trying to set up a life here and the heartbreaking sacrifices Amma made to follow him. From as early as I can remember, I knew my parents worked hard, and I believed that preserving their happiness was my responsibility.

Part of this, I discovered, was hiding information from Papa. When he got angry about something, he would get drunk and take his anger out on whoever was closest, so I learned to hide a lot from him. These secrets were my first indication that the currency of peace was concealing parts of my life. After receiving citizenship, it became my job to help my parents achieve their American dream. I sympathized with how hard they worked, and I could not be the one to tear down all that they had worked for. Unfortunately, one part of me strayed away from this perfect family image.

I don't know if it was the way my hips swayed, the hand gestures I used when I talked, or the unintentional twang in my words when I got too excited in conversations, but, from a young age, I was often asked if I was gay - a question my parents promptly shut down and ignored. I immediately became self-conscious about my mannerisms. I would put my hands in my pockets when I spoke, avoid batting my eyelashes, and tighten my thighs to walk erect like a "straight" man. I felt like a clam, shutting tighter and tighter before I realized I had tightly shut away my sexuality.

All I knew was that protecting my parents' happiness and preserving my

American-Pakistani dream meant protecting them from this queer side of me.

Being gay was undesirable to my parents, so it became undesirable to me too. I knew it wasn't "normal" according to my culture, and this brewed internalized homophobia and self-rejection. I was afraid of what my father and family members might do if they found out. Sexuality was such a delicate topic, and I knew I wouldn't be approached with compassion. Instead, I would be confronted with aggressive tactics to "fix" me. I knew I was supposed to want to change, and I hoped that I could be attracted to women one day. I shut everyone out, fearing the risk of letting anyone help me, and dug myself deeper into the closet to maintain my responsibility to my parents.

Internally, this felt like a battle equivalent to the Kargil War*. Shah Rukh Khan and Vivek Oberoi, popular Bollywood actors, had been my childhood crushes for as long as I could remember. As a middle schooler, fantasizing was normal and could often be chalked up to uncontrollable hormones. However, the more I gave into my thoughts about men, the more I felt like I was regressing from the life my parents had worked so hard to build for us and the life I knew I was supposed to want. Leaning into my sexuality quickly became synonymous with remorse. I needed to control these fantasies.

I would often try to redirect my mind to actresses I saw on television or female characters I might have read about, but I always came back to men. I tried to visualize myself settling down in a nuclear family with a woman and children, living with my parents in the same large home, and eventually retiring in Pakistan, but I was unable to.

I had a girlfriend in high school, hoping that was all the proof I needed to convince others, and myself, that this was the life I wanted. It was easy to keep the relationship alive because I went to an all-boys Catholic high school, and she went to another high school pretty far away. We met at an SAT program and didn't see each other often, so it worked well for me.

One time, a friend came over after school. We were play-wrestling when he started to kiss my neck. It felt good, and I didn't stop him. I had dreamt about him doing this to me, and I could not believe it was happening. It was one of the happiest and most blissful moments of my life. We made out for a while until I noticed the hickeys he gave me. When my parents saw the hickeys that evening, they were furious, with suspicions that it was the friend that came over. I told them I had snuck out to see my girlfriend, and they seemed calmer. This reinforced my belief that I could not be out to my parents, definitely not while living with them. By that point, I had become an expert at the language, cadence, and tonality needed to hide from them.

When it was time to pick where I would spend my undergraduate years, I knew it was the responsible thing to do to stay in New York to take care of my family and protect my mother as the abuse continued. When I received a full-tuition scholarship to a small liberal arts college in Maine, choosing to attend was the most challenging decision I had ever made. Finances in our family had been tight since 9/11 and the subsequent recession, so I knew I had to accept the scholarship. A part of me was relieved to leave, but I still carried guilt about leaving my mother behind in a home ridden with anger and abuse.

In this liberal arts bubble, I began to unpack the discomfort that shaped my thoughts around identity. I started with race, exploring the structural and institutional implications of the racism my parents faced post-9/11, and I slowly began to learn about sexuality and the spectrum it fell on. I enjoyed talking about sexuality as an abstract concept and valued people being their authentic selves, but there was a block every time I tried to apply queer theory to myself. I tried to put myself on the spectrum, but "sometimes I have gay thoughts" never fit within the framework.

Bottling up my feelings for so long became exhausting and unbearable. I needed to be with a man, and I turned to the most discreet platform I could think of - *Craigslist*. I wish I could give my younger self a big hug and say, "literally try anything else."

It wasn't terrible or anything, but it was definitely not an easy transition into exploring this side of myself. I went on a few dates, some better than others. I discovered that the more withdrawn and shy the other person was, the more comfortable I would feel. I saw a reflection of myself in them, and this made me trust them. It felt safer to be with someone who was more careful around the situation. It gave me permission to test the boundaries while knowing that it would never go too far.

Slowly, I became comfortable enough to transition from "straight" to "bisexual." I didn't proclaim this to the world, but I announced it to myself, and that felt like a victory.

A few years later, still in the closet, I went to graduate school in the Midwest. Part of why I had picked this specific program was the opportunity to go abroad. As I immersed myself in a curriculum that prepared me for diversity and inclusion work in higher education, I wanted to reflect on my identities outside of US standards.

During my trip to China, I was able to think critically about my identity as a Pakistani while surrounded by my Black, Asian, and White colleagues. I thought about what it meant to be American in China. But, I continued to avoid thinking about my sexual orientation. I would sometimes catch myself scanning a room to appreciate cute guys, but other than that, nothing. One person on our trip was out, and I remember him asking our host what being gay in China looked like. Our host mentioned that gay bars existed, but they were in a specific place on the other side of town ironically named "the red light district," comparing queerness in China with the prostitution and sexual promiscuity you would find in Amsterdam. I remember feeling sad hearing about the marginalization, slowly realizing that I could not live in parts of the world. Without outrightly admitting it, I could see the closet door cracking open, little by little.

When I came back to campus, I returned to my job as a graduate administrative assistant, leading students through social identity wheels. I started to feel inauthentic. Here I was, intending to be a social justice change agent for students, facilitating activities around identity and authenticity, and I couldn't even build up the courage to express myself authentically.

I couldn't stop thinking about it, and I couldn't focus on my academic work anymore. I felt disconnected from the people around me as I wrangled with this discomfort. I knew that if I stayed in the closet, I wouldn't make it professionally or personally.

I had a meeting set up with my independent study professor to explain why I wasn't keeping up with the work. That was the first time I told someone that I was gay. Hearing it come out of my mouth was a euphoric and startling moment. I needed to practice saying it, so I ran to a friend's place to say it again. And then another friend's place to say it again. I wanted to hear it echoing all around me. I finally felt relief.

I developed a five-year plan to tell Amma. All these years later, I still felt guilty for leaving her in that abusive environment, and I didn't want to risk her safety by telling Papa. My plan was initially to tell her I wasn't interested in marriage but that I would eventually marry and marry a woman. Then, I would tell her that I was not thinking about marriage yet, and I didn't know when I would be. The next year, I would say I wasn't interested in a family because I wanted to focus on my education. I would keep it going, assessing how the previous stages went, before deciding if I wanted to come out. Each time I went home for a semester break, I would practice the "relaxed" body language and facial expressions I had specialized in all these years to combat any questions she had. I had been playing the role all my life, and it almost felt automatic.

However, the five-year plan soon turned into a six-month plan.

Amma and I had a New Year's Eve tradition of eating *golgappa*, a savory South Asian street food, as we watched the ball drop. That year, the conversation came up again.

"Why aren't you interested in getting married?"

"I want to focus on academics, and marriage isn't on my mind."

"Are you interested in women?"

I paused. "No."

"What about men?"

"Yes." I don't know if it was the comfort of sharing this ritual experience with her or the tenderness in her voice that made me open up, but I knew I just needed to be honest.

We spent the rest of the night talking about boys that I was kind of seeing and laughing about it all before going to bed.

But, when I saw her the next morning, it seemed to have all finally hit her. She looked lost, like the light had been cast out of her eyes. I didn't know how to help her process this new me, but I knew she needed help. I did my best to be supportive, but when she shared that her biggest worry was what *Allah* might do, I didn't know what to say.

I tried my best to explain that God made me this way, so He must love me exactly as I am. I offered resources about sexuality and gay sex, and she seemed receptive to learning more.

She ended our conversation with, "every family has their problem, and this is ours." I rephrased it as, "this isn't a problem. We are finding a solution to the problem we had before." We worked together to get through it, mainly because she never shut me down.

Through our discussions, she realized that I didn't need to change. And I realized that she didn't need saving. Amma explained the trauma she faced in her relationship with my father and why her choices made sense for her. Although I took the role of "man of the house" at a young age, she assured me that it was her role as the parent to look after the child. I felt like a butterfly finally breaking free from a cocoon that was no longer mine. It was time for me to let go of the responsibility I thrust onto myself to protect my family and trust my mother to protect herself.

Returning to campus after this conversation, I felt empowered to stop hiding my feminine side that I had rejected for so long, but it was a journey. The first time I painted my nails, I remember looking down at my hairy knuckles and toes and crying because it didn't look right. I knew I needed to work on that, not only because I needed to be open to identities outside of gender binaries within the scope of my job but also because I craved victory against the internalized homophobia that kept me from seeing my own attractiveness.

I decided to ask a friend to help me paint my nails. Although I already knew how to do it, I wanted a safe environment with someone I trusted to get excited about expressing myself. We found fun colors and discovered the beauty in mixing and blending femininity and masculinity.

I pierced my ear and alternated studs and dangly chandelier earrings. I wore gold lipstick and eye make-up to parties with friends and took baby steps to move forward. I freed my hands from my pockets and began to use the gestures I wanted to use to punctuate my point, and I was finally comfortable winding my waist when I danced with friends.

Coming out in other parts of my life made me feel liberated to come out about everything, including my religion. I began questioning the religion that I was raised with and the religion I was taught in Catholic school. Questions I had as a teenager surfaced, and I started to reflect on the interconnectedness of my ethnicity, sexuality, and religion.

I had conversations with friends about the existence of hell given the kindness of God and the perceptions of heaven that seemed to be so humanly constructed. While Amma taught me that *Allah* encouraged people to question things, as I challenged these beliefs, I worried that *Allah* would punish me for even questioning His existence.

I went to a couple of conferences that highlighted queer people of color, and specifically the queer Asian American experience. I met queer South Asians, queer Pakistanis, and queer Muslims for the first time. I saw my first South Asian drag queen and learned about a retreat on the intersection of Islam and sexuality. The retreat made me question my relationship with religion even further. I began to identify as a questioning Muslim rather than a practicing Muslim. It became increasingly clear that I needed an agnostic space for further exploration. But, seeing role models and examples of people that looked like me still felt so encouraging.

This representation, which was once so hidden to me, helped me recognize my agency in questioning what I was once meant to accept and believe. I also recognize Amma's agency in making decisions that work for her without needing my saving. One by one, I have begun making choices that pushed me away from taking responsibility for the happiness at home.

I used to believe it was selfish to take care of myself and put myself first, but it can be so taxing to invest in others without investing in yourself. I have started collecting more make-up and practicing tutorials on YouTube. I have sixteen new pairs of dangly earrings, and I plan to shake my head a lot while wearing them because what's the point otherwise. I have friends to discuss my challenging religious views with and embrace being Agnostic and Muslim. I have come to terms with my gay identity. I know that if my younger self could see me now, he would be so proud. I wish he could see the possibility of what he could be one day.

Contributor's Bio:

Adan Hussain (he/him) was born in Pakistan and grew up in Queens, New York. He was raised Muslim while he attended Lutheran and Catholic K-12 schools. He went to a small liberals arts school for college and got his master's in Higher Education and Student Affairs. Adan has been working in diversity, and equity, and inclusion roles for nearly 12 years. From facilitating conversations on race as a student volunteer to serving first-generation students, Adan has pursued a career centered around social identities and how students make meaning of themselves.

Beyond the Binaries

Samia
as told to Editor

I was fifteen years old when my father got a new job in Georgia and moved us from the greater Toronto area to a suburb of Atlanta. We settled into an apartment but later decided to move into a house. As we packed up the apartment, sorting through books and clothes and papers, I picked up a heap of documents to look through. As I sifted through the documents, a stack of photos fell out. I bent over to pick them up when I noticed that all the photos were of me just after I had been born. I had never seen pictures of myself that young. As I shuffled through, I saw a photo of a woman, a stranger, holding me. Confused, I held up the photograph to my father, standing across from me.

"Who is this woman? I've never seen her before."

As I held up the photo to face him, I realized there was writing on the back. It said, "Samia, this is me holding you when you were three days old. Love, your birth mother."

Shocked, I asked, "I'm adopted?" My father's face went grey. My mother burst into tears.

"Yes," my father finally said.

As my mother explained why they had kept it a secret from me all these years, something about her fear that I would leave them, I tried to process what had just happened. I started asking questions about where my birth mother was from, who my birth father was, and why I was put up for adoption. They didn't know anything about my birth father, but they told me that my birth mother was Egyptian.

At the time, I didn't feel angry or frustrated that they had kept this from me. I initially felt shocked and confused, though the anger found its way to me years later. Adoption agencies back in the early 90s often told parents not to immediately tell their children about the adoption because they believed that would help them integrate into their adopted families better. Frankly, I wonder if they would have ever told me I was adopted had I not found out myself. My parents viewed adoption as an opportunity to offer kids that might have otherwise had a difficult life, a good one. In that respect, they did a wonderful job. They just didn't realize the significance that racial identity and ethnicity hold in the west and how they can shape your identity, life, and community. They saw me, a brown child, as just that -- someone who could be just like them and assimilate into their culture without any issue.

I did, however, feel angry and hurt that I wasn't able to be immersed in my cultural roots until much later in my life. And even then, I felt like a stranger looking from the outside in.

My skin is golden-brown, and I passed relatively easily as South Asian for the majority of my life. Additionally, I was raised with South Asian culture. I grew up eating *chaat* with my cousins and being forced to wear a *salwar kameez*, to family get-togethers. But, when I was 12 or 13 years old, I remember going to my cousin's wedding and asking a family member why I "looked different" from the rest of my family. I could never quite put my finger on it, but I always felt different.

After I found out that I was adopted, I rejected my South Asian ancestry for years. I identified only as Egyptian and didn't even mention that I was raised by South Asian parents. And yet, I didn't feel quite Egyptian either; I didn't speak the language, didn't know anything about the culture. I felt so confused.

When I eventually met my birth mother, it was like meeting a total stranger. We first met in the US, even though she and my half-sister still lived in Cairo. As overwhelming as that experience was, and as many emotions as it brought up, it couldn't parallel the first time I went to Egypt. Feeling like a foreigner in my own land was such a difficult experience. I slowly began piecing together the different parts of my identity.

On this second trip to meet her, my birth mother finally told me more about my birth father. She told me he was from the Swahili coast in East Africa, but he was Omani. She told me his ancestry was both African and Arab. And when I was in Egypt, people consistently perceived me as an African Arab for the first time in my life. So late in life, I came face to face with all of my identities -- Arab, North African, East African, and South Asian. I couldn't wrap my head around where I fit in. My birth mother told me I was Arab and Black by ancestry, but I had not been raised with these cultures or experiences. And at the same time, I didn't feel truly South Asian. I knew more about my identity at this age than I had ever known before, and yet I had never felt so lost.

I attended Arab events, but I never felt like I belonged there. I attended Black events but felt like I should not be taking up space there. Black people in the U.S. face such a specific set of struggles that I never experienced growing up. I still don't experience these struggles, as I'm seen as non-Black most of the time. I didn't want to act as though I had these experiences that I didn't, but I didn't know where I belonged. Ultimately, it took me years to come to terms with how I identify racially and ethnically. I am culturally South Asian, raised South Asian, and my family is South Asian. So, I am South Asian. But my ancestry and roots are Egyptian, Omani, and coastal East African. I hold all of these complex identities, and this makes me who I am. People have always struggled with the in-between and nuance of identities, and so did I. Being adopted made it all so much more confusing.

When I was in Egypt, my birth mother told me that adoption was a foreign concept. When she gave me up for adoption, the only two options for children born out of wedlock were to be left at the steps of a mosque or killed. If they survived, they wouldn't be given a last name since Arab lineage is passed down through the father, thus marking them for life as children that had been abandoned.

Learning about my alternate fate as a child growing up in Egypt made me think about all the different paths my life could have taken. Would I feel more complete by being connected to my birth culture and being able to speak Arabic, or less complete from being branded as an abandoned child? As a queer, non-binary person, I wondered: would I have been able to come to terms with my sexuality and gender identity if I had grown up there? It was hard enough having grown up where I did.

I remember the first time I felt attracted to a woman. I was ten years old, watching our mosque's yearly talent show when I saw a woman dancing on the stage. I stood up from my seat and couldn't stop staring. I had this weird feeling in the pit of my stomach that shot up my spine and raised the hairs all over my body. The feeling felt nice but wrong. I was so shaken up by the feeling that I sat back down. I knew I wasn't supposed to feel that way, even though I didn't even know what the feeling was at the time. Years later, I realized that it was attraction.

When I was 13, I came out quietly to myself as bisexual, but I felt such overwhelming shame and guilt and fear that I went right back into the closet a few days later. Throughout my high school years, I experienced attraction to girls, and I suppressed it, deeper and deeper. Finally, in my first semester of freshman year in college, encouraged by a close gay friend, I accepted that I was attracted to women. And only a few weeks later, I came out as a lesbian.

This period of my life was so, so difficult for me. I had an incredibly challenging time accepting myself as a queer person, especially as I was raised Muslim, and an only, adopted child. The burden of my parents' hopes and beliefs, and expectations felt like they were placed squarely on my shoulders. I worried that I would disappoint them, that they would regret adopting me because I turned out this way. It was a dark time for me, and I struggled with alcohol and substance abuse as I tried to forget my fears and worries.

At the time, I was at a predominantly white institution (PWI), which made things much more difficult. I didn't know any queer Muslim people; I had no role models to look up to, no idea of what my life could be like. Surrounded by white LGBTQ people, I was told by a gay friend that I must come out to everyone in my life, that this was a rite of passage for all LGBTQ people. If I didn't come out to my parents, then I was just hiding in the closet. They breezily said that if their parents didn't accept them, they would just stop talking to them. This just didn't feel right to me. It felt so antithetical to my upbringing as a South Asian; most South Asian kids I knew hid things from their parents, whether they were queer or not. Still, influenced by white LGBTQ culture, I didn't want to be seen as fearful or closeted. So, I decided to come out to my mom. She took it as well as a South Asian parent could and told me that she loved me regardless, but I still felt so guilty.

As I further entered the queer community, I realized there were unspoken rules about gender. I came out in 2010 when it felt like the gender roles in the queer community were almost as rigid as those in the straight community -- you could be a "stud/butch," a "femme," or a "stemme" (somewhere right in the middle). Since at the time, I wore tight clothes, liked makeup, and enjoyed wearing heels, I figured I must be a femme. And if you were a femme, you mostly dated studs. So that's what I did. The more studs I dated, the more I felt pushed into the category of "femme." Many of the studs I dated were controlling and felt threatened by any masculinity I tried to display. I started dressing up a little more masculine behind their backs and realized I liked it. Later, when I began dating femmes, I felt more empowered to experiment with my gender expression.

In 2013, the terms "queer" and "non-binary" began becoming more mainstream within the LGBTQ community. It felt like we were all expanding how we looked at gender and what it meant to be gender non-conforming. I remember the first person I knew who was non-binary -- a friend who came out to me and asked me to use "they/them" pronouns to refer to them. This was the first time I had ever heard of anyone using pronouns other than "she" or "he." This was so eye-opening for me. It felt revolutionary, like anything was possible. I realized that none of those rigid gender categories mattered.

As I felt freer to experiment with my gender, I became more and more fluid. I would switch back and forth between feminine and masculine expressions from day to day, depending on how I felt when I woke up that morning. But as I leaned more into my masculinity, I felt increasingly uncomfortable with the way my naturally curvy body looked in men's clothing. It never felt like anything fit, and I had multiple (embarrassing) meltdowns in the men's section of clothing stores. I had a conversation with a non-binary friend, who identified that what I was feeling was gender dysphoria*. Naming these feelings was both comforting and terrifying. It felt like I was constantly changing.

In 2015, I got my first binder* from that same friend. The first time I put it on, I was completely overwhelmed looking at myself in the mirror. I kept running my hand over my mostly flat chest and marveled at how immediately confident I felt in my masculine expression. And even then, the slight bump of my breasts beneath the binder bothered me. Slowly, I also began asking friends to refer to me using "they/them" pronouns. The first time a friend used my pronouns, I felt so seen and visible. It wasn't the pronoun so much that made me feel this way, but the feeling of someone else affirming me for who I was.

In 2017, I moved to DC for a Ph.D. program and discovered that I was the first non-binary student they had ever had. When I moved, I decided to begin using "they/them" pronouns exclusively as a step forward in coming into my own gender identity. This was a major struggle and adjustment for some of the other students and all of the faculty members. We weren't at the point where pronouns were seamlessly integrated into introductions, and I was nervous every time I had to correct someone. It felt like I was coming out e very single day.

At this point, I was wearing binders regularly and wanted to wear them almost all of the time, but I couldn't because of how much they hurt my back. I was already six feet tall and worried about back problems; the prospect of being hunched over in old age scared me. I decided only to wear binders when I felt like my back could handle it and suffered through gender dysphoria the rest of the time. Sometimes I would have consecutive days or weeks of intense dysphoria, and I would wear binders daily until the dysphoria decreased. Taking the binder off at the end of these days felt both liberating and sad.

One day, I was talking to an ex-partner about my dysphoria when they asked me if I had ever considered getting top surgery*. I had considered it but was afraid that having no breasts altogether would alter my femme expression in a way I wasn't sure about. They asked if I had considered getting a breast reduction instead; to help reduce my dysphoria in my masculine expression but still have breasts in my femme expression. I had never thought about this before, and the idea ignited something in me. The more I thought about the possibility of smaller breasts and less dysphoria, the more and more I wanted it.

I began researching the possibility of getting a breast reduction: how much it would cost, what it would entail, whether insurance covered it. I discovered that breast reductions counted as gender-affirming surgeries, which were covered by my health insurance at the time. The possibility of getting one felt all the more real for me.

As the surgery became more of a reality, I grappled with whether I wanted a breast reduction or full top surgery. I wondered whether I would get a reduction and then, still stuck having to wear bras and binders, regret not having gotten a full removal. I considered why I felt so afraid of getting rid of my breasts altogether and how my attachment to having breasts in order to present as femme could be internalized transphobia.

I decided to schedule a consultation at a local LGBTQ clinic and see what they said. I asked them about the possibility of getting a breast reduction now and getting full top surgery later, if I eventually decided that I wanted a full removal. They explained that I would only be able to receive one gender-affirming top surgery (reduction or removal) covered by insurance, even if I changed insurance. This shifted things for me. I worried that I would regret getting a reduction and not a full removal. I told them I needed some time to think about it and that I would be in touch soon.

I began looking into the possibility of full top surgery more and more. I was scrolling through the #topsurgery hashtag on *Instagram*, trying to figure out what surgery I really wanted and what top surgery scars would look like on brown skin. Suddenly, I came across an account of a non-binary person who had gotten top surgery but dressed femme most of the time. This was precisely the representation I needed to make up my mind. Of course, I knew that people without breasts could present as femme and look incredible; but I always worried that I would not. Seeing the visual representation of what I could look like was life-changing for me. It showed me in a very concrete way that I could get top surgery, feel comfortable in my body, and dress however I wanted to, whenever I wanted to. I had made up my mind.

I called the clinic and scheduled a full top surgery for two months later, just five days after my 27th birthday. The time went by incredibly fast. I put together my care team, who would support me in the two weeks after I got surgery, as I would be on pain medication and unable to do most things for myself. I watched innumerable YouTube videos on what surgery aftercare looked like. After feeling so out of control about who I was, where I came from, and who I wanted to be, it felt comforting to have some say in who I would become.

During those two months, I considered whether I should tell my parents about the surgery. I was not out to them as non-binary, mostly because I didn't think they would know what that meant, even if I tried to explain it to them. I felt that it almost would have been easier if I was a trans man because at least they would understand me "wanting to be a man." My "in-between" had always confused them.

When I began dressing masculine, allowing myself to have body hair, and cutting my hair short, my mom was shocked. She asked me if I wanted to be a man, to which I replied I did not. When I came out to her as a lesbian, she hadn't minded as much because I still dressed femme and could go to family functions without raising any eyebrows. But as my outward expression began to change, she realized she could no longer hide my gender or sexuality from the extended family. She would admonish me to shave my legs, wear makeup, and wear feminine clothing around the family. In the beginning, I relented to appease her, but over time I stood stronger in who I was. We constantly fought when it came to the family, and she even told me that she would rather me not come to family functions than attend dressed how I was. I knew that the very visible change of removing my breasts would hurt her because she would have no idea how to explain it to our family members. I ultimately decided not to tell them beforehand because I was worried they would try to convince me not to do it. I was already in a precarious state, preparing for a life-changing surgery, and I didn't want the additional stress.

On October 28, 2019, I got top surgery. The total recovery was a difficult, long six weeks, during which I couldn't lift my arms above shoulder level. The first two weeks, I had to rely almost entirely on my friends and housemates to complete basic chores and tasks for me. After the first week, I went to the surgeon for a check-up to ensure everything was healing okay. This was the first time I saw my chest. I looked down at the expanse of my completely flat chest and could not believe my eyes.

My parents had been asking me to come down for a visit throughout my recovery and afterward, but I stalled as long as I could. A few months after my surgery, I went to see them when I felt well enough to visit. I knew I would have to tell both of my parents during the visit, but I decided to tell my dad first. I wasn't sure how to phrase the conversation. Still, I ultimately decided to focus on my decision to get surgery as something that would make me feel more comfortable in my body, rather than focusing on my identity as non-binary. It was a very awkward conversation at first because, like most Desi fathers, he did not want to think about my body at all, let alone my breasts. I told him I decided to remove my breasts because it made me feel more comfortable with myself. We went back and forth a few times, and although I kept trying to explain it to him, it still seemed like he didn't understand.

A few months earlier, I had given him a copy of Arundhati Roy's new book, *The Ministry of Utmost Happiness*. While this book had received many valid criticisms, I thought my dad would enjoy it since he loved Indian history and fiction. One of the book's main characters is a member of a third gender group in India, neither male nor female. I knew my dad had heard of and met other people from this gender group before, having grown up in Pakistan. In having the conversation about my surgery, he brought up the book, even though I had not brought up my trans identity. He said, "I don't know what it's like to live the way you live. I can imagine it's complicated for you, and I can't judge you for any of the choices you make that make it easier for you to live in this world. Like I'm reading in the book, I can't judge her for her choices, and like that, I can't judge you." The connection that he independently drew between my surgery and my gender identity was heartwarming. While he still didn't fully understand the grey area, he was trying, and he didn't judge me, and that was all I could ask for.

Later that evening, I sat my mom down and told her, too. She asked if I had gotten bottom surgery as well and wanted to be a man. I told her no, but I didn't have the words to explain my non-binary identity to her, so I just left it at that. She ultimately accepted my decision as much as she could and loved me, still.

Top surgery has been both a challenging and rewarding experience for me. After I got the surgery, I felt like I had gone through such an immense shift. I had literally altered my body to look and feel closer to how I saw myself. So when I went out into the world and continued to be gendered as a woman almost all of the time, it hurt more than ever before. The realization that I was still not being seen in the way that I saw myself increased my dysphoria considerably. I began wanting to take testosterone more and more. But I had promised myself that I wouldn't make any significant shifts to my body for at least one year after the surgery to allow this massive change to settle in, so I ultimately decided not to take T. Over time, the increased dysphoria settled down, and I integrated my sense of self with how my body looked now. I reminded myself that the world would never truly see me, neither in the fullness of my non-binary identity nor in the complexity of my racial and ethnic identities. But that doesn't take away from who I truly am.

I am South Asian and multiracial and Arab and African and non-binary, some days all at once and some days to differing degrees. I care less than I ever have about how other people perceive me. And finally, I can look in the mirror and like what I see. Finally, I can get dressed in the morning without deciding between back pain and gender alignment.

Finally, my body fits how I see myself, and ultimately, this is what matters. That is peace.

I am still figuring out how all these pieces of my identity integrate into who I am. I feel more at peace with my gender, ethnic, and racial identity now than I ever have before, but I still sometimes struggle, as we all do. I am, finally, fiercely committed to being myself and to holding all of my experiences and identities in their fullness. I exist in the in-between, and that is a beautiful thing.

Contributor's Bio:

Samia (any/all pronouns) is a queer, genderfluid facilitator, advocate, and creator. They currently work with queer & trans youth, imagining new worlds for them to inhabit. She is the co-creator of the Transform Gender Collective, a community for transmasculine and masculine-of-center Black, Indigenous, and people of color (BIPOC) to explore support, accountability, and transformative justice. You can find him sharing food and thoughts with loved ones, dreaming about liberation, and sipping lots of tea.v

How I Float

Chandani Weirsba

I'm in a committed, monogamous relationship with a straight man. Does that make our relationship straight?

On the first or second date with my now-boyfriend, I told him that I was queer. I don't remember how it came out, but I do remember thinking that it was important to tell him even before we were exclusive, and that I better tell him sooner rather than later. Waiting until I found the perfect time or way felt like I was keeping it from him; it felt deliberate, almost shady, even though I had nothing to hide. Not to mention, sharing a little about your exes is a pretty common conversation starter in the early days of a budding relationship.

This coming out experience was relatively nonchalant. I don't even remember how he initially reacted. Later, though, he did ask a lot of questions, which I answered thoroughly (better to hear it from me than from someone else). *Have you ever been in a relationship with a woman? When did you know? Does your family know? What's the difference between queer and bisexual?* And of course, *have you ever had sex with a woman?* Hearing his questions and revisiting memories of queer relationships and encounters reaffirmed that I was, in fact, queer, and he was definitely straight.

We went through a similar process on our first date for my "coming out" as biracial; half Desi, half white. He told me that his way of figuring out if I were white was to see how I responded when he complimented my lengha – a traditional South Asian outfit – in my dating profile. I showed him pictures of me and my family, and he asked questions about my upbringing. These questions were pretty standard for any of my previous first dates, so I was relatively unfazed. We laughed over comparing and explaining foods important to each of our cultures and our families' cooking. I elaborated on the many Indian-Hindu weddings I had been to and the close relationships I had with cousins, *mosis* (maternal aunts), and my *nani* and *nana* (maternal grandparents).

When I'm surrounded by people who know me, I float through my day. I don't have to explain who or what I am; I'm not forced to change how I present myself. When I help my mom make a *sabji* (vegetable dish) or text my sister and her name pops up on my phone screen as "*Didi*" (older sister), I don't think twice. Going to my nani's house for *roti* and *sabji* or choreographing a dance for a cousin's *sangeet* (pre-wedding event) comes as second nature.

Sometimes, with colleagues, strangers, or on the street, I don't float. I'm forced to think more carefully about how others interpret everything about me. I change how I explain myself, and I choose my words with caution to make sure that I'm not misinterpreted. In these moments, I live and act as a person defined by the way she looks. It can be frustrating and even nerve-racking going on dates, being interviewed, and meeting new people. Because I present as white, I know I'll have to explain my background one way or another, if only to ease their confusion about my name or justify why my opinion or experience might be relevant.

I eat *dahl chaval* (lentils and rice) every week and want to be able to pleat my own *sari*. My box of *bindis* (both my multicolored fancy ones and maroon ones for *Bharatanatyam performances*) is next to my nail polish. One of my favorite pairs of earrings is a set of gold, black, and white *jumkhis* that my *mosi* brought back from India. I've dreamt of my wedding dress – a gem-studded, sparkly, color-scheme-to-be-determined *lengha*.

Even if these weren't part of my experience – although it's hard to imagine my life any other way – I would still be biracial, and my identification would be more complicated and nuanced than my looks suggest. The food, clothes, language, and culture all floats in my mind and through my body each and every day. It's part of what makes me uniquely me.

I also float through the day as a queer woman. My queerness is newer to me than my biracial-ness; my flight pattern is a little uneven. Sometimes I question it; sometimes others make assumptions about it. After all, I'm in a relationship with a straight man, and even if I weren't, most people don't know that I'm queer.

I started seriously thinking about my queerness the summer after my freshman year of college, after my first heartbreak and a few months before my close cousin and her now-wife got married. Until that point, I floated through each day, not stopping to reflect on my sexuality. Leading up to my cousin's marriage, I thought more and more about who I had been attracted to and what sort of attraction it was. I started viewing attractionality as more varied and nuanced than I had ever before. I analyzed sexual and physical attraction, romantic and emotional attraction, and realized that I had felt some of these different types of attraction for women before.

When I was younger, I dreamed of being like Sonali Bendre from *Hum Saath Saath*

Hain. I loved her shy smile, her long, dark hair, and perhaps most of all, her nose ring. I wanted one just like hers. I liked some of the men in the movie too, but I also cared for her. I thought she was so beautiful. I'd watch her dance (or shyly hide her face, as she did frequently) in "Mhare Hiwada Mein" over and over. I wanted to dance to "Maiyya Yashoda" at my own sangeet.

I felt similarly about Kareena Kapoor in "San Sanana" from *Asoka*. I thought she looked sexy, dancing under the flowing water and rising out of the river, barely clothed and soaking wet, with her long hair clinging to her back and shoulders. I imitated her by re-wetting my hair after a shower, letting it stay dark and soaking wet as I ran my fingers through it and danced in my underwear.

I spent hours as a teenager on YouTube, watching Rihanna dance in "SOS." I loved watching her body move in the tight, green dress, making her cleavage more pronounced. I thought she looked hot with bangs, and the shimmery oil that coated her skin made it look radiant. I imagined myself dancing alongside her.

My mind wanders back to these celebrities I once spent hours poring over. I can't find a specific moment in time that I knew my attraction to beautiful women was more than just admiration. For me to gain a semblance of clarity, it took *Tinder* matches and *HER* dates, first kisses and cuddles, relationships and sex. It took uncomfortable conversations, uncertainty, and a lot of time reflecting on my own. It took courage and support from siblings and friends. It also took freedom, the sort of space I had in college to generally do what I wanted, when, and with whom I chose. That freedom – to begin to date who and how I wanted with few negative consequences from my generally unaware parents – was key in me grounding my queer identity.

There are times I go through my day and am gently reminded of my queerness, whether it's through a conversation at work, an assumption being made about my or someone else's romantic life, or seeing a Pride flag off the side of the street. There are other times when I feel decidedly straight. These are most often times when I'm with my boyfriend or around couples I assume are straight. Sometimes I think that he forgets that I'm queer; at other times, he'll surprise me by casually bringing it up in a conversation. Although I most often remind him of my queerness with one-off remarks, I sometimes question myself. *Am I actually queer? Was that just a college phase, like everyone claims some girls go through? Could I ever love a woman the way I love him?*

I feel a sense of inauthenticity identifying as queer because I'm in a relationship with a man. I don't feel the same way identifying as mixed. While I can't determine how others perceive my racial identity (even Desis don't get the hint when they see or hear my name), I do have a choice about who I date and how I present as a feminine queer woman. In a world where your romantic relationships build up a public, incomplete image of you, I have to remind myself that relationships and appearance don't make or break my queerness. I'm queer with or without a queer relationship. I'm biracial with or without looking racially ambiguous. Without these reminders, my floating gets shaky.

I went through college and the years since, dating both women and men, catching feelings and letting crushes bud into romances a few times over. I became more comfortable with my sexual experiences while also becoming comfortable with my sexual identity. I've been shaped by the strong Desi women around me. I've also been influenced by the media and my girl fantasies of an Indian-Hindu wedding in which my groom would twirl me at our *sangeet*; I'd float around the dance floor as my jewel-studded *lengha* sailed through the air. There was a period of time when I realized that my fantasy might not come true. It surprised me more than anything. My heart and mind adapted to embrace a new possibility: marrying a woman. I could still have my *sangeet* and a jewel-studded *lengha*.

In the end, I have ownership over my story. Like most people, the way I identify to both myself and others has changed over time. Even if I didn't technically have crushes on Sonali Bendre or Rihanna, reflecting on my attraction to them led me to discover more about myself.

I float through each day surrounded by people who love and respect me, who trust that I don't take advantage of my privilege and know that I'm being authentically me. I don't assert or push away my identities just when it suits me. Instead, I offer space to those who can't always be their authentic selves and connect with them through our shared experiences. I may go through life being forced to "out" my biracial-ness or my queerness, and that's okay. Occasionally I might feel guilty or less secure in my identities, but I have a community that will lift me into the air. And off I'll go, floating steadily once more.

Contributor's Bio:

Chandani Wiersba (she/her) identifies as biracial, mixed, and a Desi queer woman; she's half white and half Indian. Chandani uses writing to reflect on her experiences and has enjoyed performing her pieces in monologue shows and open mic nights. Her writing on identity and relationships has evolved as her perspectives on herself and the world change.

The Beauty of Brown

Bristi
as told to Editor

I was five years old the first time someone showed me that being brown was not beautiful. I was in kindergarten and still vividly remember a fellow student pulling on my long, black hair and asking me where my bow and arrow was. Obviously, they were referring to Indigenous Americans, who were incorrectly dubbed "Indians" by white colonizers. When I told Mama what happened after school, she set up a meeting with my teacher. I'm still not sure what happened during that meeting, but Mama came home the following evening and told Baba that what had happened to me was racist. I had no clue what that meant at the time; all I knew was that being brown was worthy of ridicule.

My family and I moved to Pennsylvania the following year. In a suburb dominated by lemonade stands and cookie sales, the fragrance of tandoori spices and fresh elaichi poured out of our house. The bullying continued. Before I could comprehend what made our glittery clothing, aromatic dishes, and tongue-twisting language special, I knew that it was safer to reject it.

I remember seeing other Indian kids be teased about the same oil my Mama would lovingly massage into my hair. From then on, I pushed her oily hands away anytime she went near my scalp.

One time, Baba forced me to wear a red embroidered *Anarkali* dress to a Christmas concert my orchestra put on because I didn't have any other festive red dresses to wear. I threw a tantrum and begged him to let me change, but we were already late. I walked into the auditorium hall, my body stiff and my breath fast, and heard all my peers snickering. One group boldly erupted in laughter, pointing at my dress as I walked past them.

It wasn't the teasing itself that bothered me. I was okay with being teased for choices that I had some control over, like wearing hand-me-downs or being a tomboy. But, being South Asian, being brown, was not a choice. It was the color of the skin I was born into. I remember my parents' confusion and exhaustion with my stubborn hatred for the culture they worked so hard to preserve in this foreign country. I remember practicing American phrases in the mirror because, even though I was born here and English is my first language, the Bangla I spoke at home warped my accent. I remember coming home and scrubbing my arms with Clorox bleach until I bruised and bled, attempting to free myself from the color that unfairly labeled me "weird."

At the beginning of high school, I joined the 20% of American teens that suffer from depression. I had no friends, copious amounts of self-hatred for my brownness, and spent my evenings listening to my parents, trapped in a loveless marriage, fight. When my sister was diagnosed with thyroid cancer, it stimulated depressive symptoms that impacted her mood and behavior. They were similar to what I was experiencing, so Baba decided that if I had depression, it had to be genetic, and he got me tested. When my results came back negative for thyroid tests, he threatened the authenticity of my depression and told me to "never pull shit like this again."

It was around this time that I met Natalie. I texted her on the first day of school to see if we had any classes together since she was the only friend that I knew from middle school attending this high school. Natalie and I decided to have lunch together, and soon enough, she introduced me to the beautiful world of *Tumblr* and "gay ships"* within fandoms*. This became my escape.

Now, before you get ahead of yourself, Natalie and I are just friends. Aside from the multiple-hour long make-out session, we shared once to break both of our "kissing virginities," we have never crossed the *romantic* line. Rather, the shared experience of having intrusive parents who limited our self-exploration brought us together as friends. We would turn to *Tumblr* to investigate and frequently overanalyze our emotional and sexual feelings. For the first time, I began to reflect on my mental health and seek out resources. I also began to think about my sexuality. I learned about queer-coded characters, joined many fandoms, and initiated honest and vulnerable conversations with queer individuals on *Tumblr* whom I didn't personally know without the fear of backlash.

Strangely, amidst all of the bullying for the color of my skin, discovering my sexuality felt like the easy part. In time I was out almost everywhere - online and at school - and no one batted an eye. It felt weird sometimes to see how out and proud my white friends were with their families, and I was kind of jealous, but as my friend group became more racially diverse and queer, I felt prouder of my unique journey.

I was doing well, texting Natalie about Kate McKinnon by night and slowly introducing queer television shows to Mama by day to soften her up to my big gay reveal, whenever that would be. We made sure to do this while Baba was out of the house to avoid triggering his wrath. Mama is liberal and much more accepting, while Baba is close-minded when it comes to queerness, to say the least. Mama and I talk about issues that the LGBTQIA+ community faces and about television characters that were probably gay - our favorite was Elena from One Day at a Time. Once, Mama asked me to help her adjust the syllabus for the English class she teaches to be more inclusive and respectful for all sexualities and gender identities. On the other hand, Baba terrified me with mentions of abandonment, should I ever mention queerness in his home again. Baba and my conversations about queerness always end with his threats of abuse. The closer I got to my Mama, and the more I embraced my queer identity, the further I drifted from Baba and the tenser our relationship grew to be. But, Mama and I were in a good spot and, while I wasn't out to her yet, I felt content in my sexuality.

Then, college happened.

In my first semester at Penn State, I barely got out of bed, rarely attended classes, and lost fifteen pounds (so much for the 'freshman fifteen!'). My grades and physical appearance suffered, and it was clear my depression had crept back. Besides the fact that it wasn't my first choice school, it felt like all the rainbow-filled dreams I had had about college weren't real. I don't know why I expected to have a girlfriend as soon as I got to campus or why I felt like people would just know I was gay, but it felt like I was in the closet around friends for the first time. I joined an Indian classical dance team, and it felt weird to be around so many Indian people. My sister was on a dance team when she was in college, and following in her footsteps seemed like the natural thing to do. But being on the team felt constricting and suffocating.

I didn't feel like I could be myself because I knew the homophobic views brown parents, like Baba, often instill in their children. I had had such a positive experience with my queerness in high school, and I didn't want to ruin it by coming out to the only people surrounding me at the time. Eventually, just before competitions started in the spring, I decided it was time to tell them. And, honestly, that turned everything around for the better. I found endless support, and I found community.

Late-night practices and study sessions with the dance team became the reason I got out of bed. They gave me pride in my Indian heritage, introduced me to our culture's beauty, and shared anything they interpreted as the queer coding of sexuality within religious texts.

Bharatanatyam, the traditional dance form our team practiced, tends to be intrinsically linked with Hinduism, so we discussed religion often. Our dances are an iteration of famous scriptural stories told through movement and facial expressions. *Bharatanatyam* is often used to showcase devotion to Hindu Gods and Goddesses and was originally performed in temples and courts. Discussing *Bharatanatyam* and religion with these girls was the first time I could stretch the bounds of my understanding of Hinduism.

I grew up learning about Hinduism from our family's monthly trip to the temple or the cartoons many Indian Americans grow up watching. After my sister was diagnosed with cancer, I ultimately rejected the idea of God. And, knowing the complicated relationship religion often has with gayness, I repelled it even more. However, these girls taught me about the beauty of spirituality and the lessons of the Hindu religion. In the years before I joined, the dance team used the traditional art form of *Bharatanatyam* to advocate for LGBTQIA+ love, illegal immigration, and mental health in their shows. Since I'd joined, we had reverted to more traditional storytelling, but I learned about *Ramayana* and *Mahabharata*, ancient Hindu epics, in a whole new light through these stories.

Most importantly, I learned that there has always been a prominent queer community within India. Prior to colonialism, the concept of the gender binary and heteronormative love wasn't legally enforced the way it was under Section 377, and people blurred the lines much as they do now. Fluidity in gender and sexuality existed and was especially visible within art forms.

In fact, the *Ardhanarishvara*, which many *Bharatanatyam* dancers grow up learning, speaks to this. The dance is androgynous, including male and female parts by merging the god Shiva and his partner Parvati. This form of Shiva literally means "totality that lies beyond duality."

Through dance, I was able to reassess my queer South Asian identity and fall in love with my brownness. Based on my understanding, many of the biases South Asian families have against sexuality and gender were a product of British colonization and its criminalization of age-old practices, not our beautiful culture.

Honestly, think about it; in a country with a population as large as India's, you're telling me everyone is straight? India is one of the most diverse countries in the world in terms of culture, cuisine, language, and religion. In fact, state to state, people, practice traditions differently. *Holi* and *Diwali*, traditional Hindu festivals, look very different in the North and the South. We, as a people, are peaceful and happy and celebratory and colorful. If that doesn't scream "gay," I don't know what does.

The intersection I began to see between my sexuality and racial identity was astounding. If anything, this helped me embrace my brownness even more. It took years to rebuild my relationship with a culture I was forced to hate, and I refused to let go.

It is interesting to look back on the moments that catapulted my perceptions of my identities. At fifteen years old, a stranger on Tumblr shared their coming out experience with me and told me that feeling confused is normal. Their compassion made me want to scream "I'm gay" from the rooftops. Yet, at five years old, I held my face in my hands, wiping away tears, while classmates taunted me for my brownness. Their cruelty had made me reject myself and my people.

Coming to terms with your sexuality is a terrifyingly raw experience for so many. I was fortunate enough to have the empathy and guidance I needed to make it beautiful. Coming to terms with your ethnicity, on the other hand, is an often-trivialized milestone. I am automatically out in my brownness from the moment I walk into a room, yet that was the most challenging identity for me to accept. I wish I had fallen in love with my culture as quickly as I did the LGBTQIA+ community. I wish I hadn't lost all those years to peers whose names I don't even remember. I wish I had the space to explore what being South Asian meant for me. But, most of all, I wish I could have loved my brown skin before someone told me it was wrong.

Contributor's Bio:

Bristi (she/her and they/them) is a 20-year-old Psychology student at Penn State University with hopes of entering the medical field. She identifies as a queer Indian-American non-binary individual who enjoys singing and music, *Bharatanatyam* dancing, film, with a passion for the overall arts. They have always been active as a Queer or Trans Person of Color (QTPOC) and hopes to continue spreading positivity and intersectional support for others in the queer community.

Oh, To Be [Perfect]

Anamika

I had my first panic attack at an *ashram*, a Hindu hermitage. There I was, minding my own business, trying to study and practice Oneness when no good, dirty, rotten I-don't-even-want-to-say-his-name somehow managed to be crowned king of America. What the fuck? I had been out of the country for less than a week, and we handed it over to this buffoon? I began hyperventilating. I couldn't breathe. I couldn't drink water. I was gasping for air, frantically trying to dial people I loved: my partner, my sister, my best friend. Finally, someone answered. My brother-from-another-mother, thank goodness for him. He picked up the phone, "What's up, jackass?" He talked me down and helped me breathe again.

"It's okay, dear," he said. "You're not responsible for the whole world."

His words tumble around my mind. "It's okay, dear. You're not responsible for the whole world." I repeat this mantra to myself whenever those feelings creep back up again. "It's okay, dear. You're not responsible for the whole world."

Looking back on the infancy of my anxiety, I can trace the threads of unease as they permeated every aspect of my life, manifesting as self-imposed expectations. Years later, they have grown into an unscalable mountain. I expect myself to take care of my partner when he's sad, not to upset or anger him. I expect myself to uphold our different cultural and religious traditions, mixing them in a perfect balance. I expect myself to meet the needs of every person in my life - my boss, our families, my friends, and our communities. I expect myself to take care of my loved ones, career, household, and finances. I expect myself to make time for activism and boldly claim my queerness, even within my seemingly heteronormative relationship. I expect myself to meet every measure of perfection I can imagine.

I expect myself to be the different *devis*, the beautiful and powerful Goddesses, that I idolized at the ages of 16, 20, and 25 -- and I'm somehow supposed to wrap up all these *devi*-versions of myself into one brain, one body, one soul. My expectations have no sense of reality—cue anxiety.

When it got to be too much, I started therapy. And my fantastically weird, chill, and eccentric Buddhist therapist reminded me that, "It's okay, dear. You're not responsible for the whole world."

Go easy on yourself. Go easy.

My therapist and I have investigated the pressure. The need, the urge, the longing to be perfect. The source of these expectations. And Goddamit, it all comes back to the fucking "gifted" school program. "You're smart. Too smart. Much smarter than the other kids. You need extra attention, extra work. We need to help you reach your potential."

That *rakshasa* (demon) of a word - potential. What I'm not, but what I could be [if only I tried harder]. What I could be [if only I applied myself]. What I could be [if I were perfect].

Those lovely little brackets were never stated, only implied. "Be perfect. If anyone can do it, it's you!" The cheerful and well-meaning manner in which these draining thoughts were spat in my direction didn't make them any less potent, any less damaging. Believing those dangerous thoughts led to this monstrous ball of anxiety that I carry with me. Believing it was important to be perfect, to be better, to be my "best" self impacted my outlook on life.

I picture it sometimes. Perfection. Utopia. Okay, I picture it a lot. And, it's beautiful.

I wake up early, get my husband out of the house, work from home and manage an infant. Everyone is happy and cared for and has the perfect wife/mom/daughter/in-law. Birthday cards are out on time, prayers chanted, meals cooked, house cleaned. Half the time, there's even a little pride flag, Ganesha* door knocker, and a white picket fence.

Whoever sold me on this dream of a life of service must have forgotten to tell me the side effects. I lost my connection to what actually brings me joy, and I live off of the praise and contentment of others instead. When people ask me what I would do if I won the lottery, I begin daydreaming of services that would save me time - so I can work better. So I can serve better. So I can be better, [closer to perfection].

I blame all my problems on lack of time. No time to attend pride events - what kind of a queer person am I? No time to attend sit-ins or work for political campaigns or attend board meetings. No time to go to the temple or tune in for satsangs. No time to write, dance, or read poetry, or paint. When I do squeeze out the time to participate, I can hardly enjoy it before I'm back in my bubble of anxiety. Those evenings, I return home to whisk around my apartment, tut-tutting at every speck of dust - and there are a lot - groaning at every project left unfinished.

The desire to be perfect percolates everything I do... and those desires don't die down. As the responsibilities increase, the desires increase, and I seem to forget about myself.

What about me? What about the parts of me that used to matter to me? I've forgotten and neglected the facets of me that used to structure my whole identity: my desi-ness, my queerness, and my stellar self-esteem in both of these realms. When did those identities just disappear, seemingly less of a priority these days?

Aren't I incredibly desi? Whatever happened to *Bharatanatyam* and *Bhagavan* (God) and Sanskrit and *pujas* (prayers)? But I don't say my prayers very often anymore. I don't light my *diya* (clay lamp) and my house doesn't smell of *agarbatti* (incense). Instead, my partner and I have fun grooving to soca and dancehall and reggaeton. He teaches me his culture's patois, and I struggle to pronounce things properly, with my soft 'd's' and rolled 'r's' from years of speaking Hindi. As we explore each other's worlds and personalities, my independent investigations get left in the past. What happened to learning my mother's mother tongue? What happened to leaning into desi-ness? My anxiety threatens to flatten me out. Without actively being desi, I'm just another American: going to work, picking up takeout, and coming home to watch *Schitt's Creek*. When did I become so... (ugh, I almost spit the word out) so... basic?

I jump to the other identity that claimed my life before marriage. Aren't I incredibly queer? Like, very queer? It's been about nine years now -- since acknowledging my queerness. But I don't kiss women very often anymore. I kiss my lovely, straight husband. It's a little bit different when your partner has a beard. And a penis. That's different too. What happened to my rainbow-colored shirts and claiming my pride and being confident? When I venture into queer communities these days, I feel pressure to be demonstrative with my queerness, as if my existence as a queer person isn't revolutionary enough. This pressure tells me that I have to claim it with my physicality to be accepted by this community. My anxiety jumps in – "here! You missed a spot! You aren't the perfect queer or ally or social justice warrior princess you were supposed to be!"

I used to feel perfectly content in my queer identity. My sexuality was so important to me. I had even found my label during my senior year of college: demi-pansexual. Such a quintessential description of the feelings that made me different from my friends, that made my crushes and first loves unique. Before I came across my label, I'd thought about using the word bisexual for years. But it never really felt right on my tongue. When I came across the word pansexual, I was elated! It meant I wasn't a party of one; there were others who felt this way. Gender and how someone identifies doesn't matter to me... it doesn't even come into the picture for me. I just love people. It felt so good to have that word on my lips, but I still used it sparingly. There was still something different about me. And I kept investigating until I found what I was looking for: demisexual. Demisexual felt like a sigh of relief. Demisexual felt like I was finally being seen like I was no longer invisible. Like my lack of crushes on celebrities and "that hot guy over there" wasn't weird or fake.

Like my accidentally falling in love with one of my best friends *again* was maybe just how I worked. I found my perfect word. And it fits so completely. And, wow, having a perfect fit in my life felt so good.

After I got married, my sexual identity slowly faded into the background. I'm not demi-pansexual so much anymore. I'm just in love with my husband. It matters less when you're in a long-term, monogamous relationship. When I am expressing my sexuality, though it still describes an aspect of myself, I'm not demi-pansexual. I'm a partner, a lover, a wife. Sexuality is an experience now, not an identity. It's not that the label doesn't matter anymore. It's just less… salient. I don't need it as much anymore. My perfect fit is with my husband, not with a word. In many ways, my longing to be perfect within my social identities was just as damaging as my longing to be perfect within my roles and relationships.

It's taken a long time not to feel like I'm betraying my queer community by not actively engaging with my sexual identity. Or my desi upbringing, for that matter, by not actively engaging with my culture or religion. But, after years with my very patient therapist, I've decided to be me, irrespective of these identities. I'm me - no qualifiers needed. I've disentangled myself from the self-imposed expectations of a specific culture or sexuality or ethnicity or race or religion.

I look back on my childhood dreams. Before they became all about perfection. I look back on those dreams of reading all day, losing myself in worlds of words and wonder. I've begun opening up my books again, not just self-improvement books. From an outsider's perspective, it appears as though I've lost my identity anyway... might as well do it on my own terms.

"It's okay, dear. You're not responsible for the whole world."

Here I am today. Just fine. Basking in the Great Okay-ness. Why didn't anyone ever tell me that it was perfectly alright if I was just fine? Perfectly alright, not being perfect.

Perhaps they did. Perhaps it was just me still chasing this fantasy. So, today, I tell my brain sweetly to "shut up." I practice my breathing techniques, open a book, and celebrate myself.

Contributor's Bio:

Anamika (she/her) means "without a name." She chose this pen name not because she doesn't see the beauty in readers making a direct connection to the author, but because she is afraid. She is slightly afraid of using her true words in a medium that anyone may get their hands on, including her loving but probably unaware family. But mostly, she is afraid of her ego. She would much rather not give it any reason to grow to a colossal, bulbous monstrosity that won't fit in her personality anymore. So, she avoids the spotlight. She sends much love to all those who choose to read her words, nonetheless

My Queer Relationship with my Queerness

Anna

Middle-school lunch was always the same.

"Oh my God, Shawn looks so cute today. Did you see him?"

"Yes, oh my God, his hair looks so good pushed back like that! But did you see Khaled's shirt - you can *so* see his muscles through it!"

"Oh my gosh, stop, he's mine!"

"Anna, did you see him?"

What.

"Anna, did you see Shawn's hair? And Khaled's muscles?"

"Anna, you never talk about your crush! Is it a secret?? Omg, is it, Abdullah? You guys would be so cute together! Are you shy?"

"No, I just don't care."

"What do you mean? Do you think boys have cooties or something? Gosh, grow up!"

I didn't, in fact, think boys had cooties. I just didn't get the hype. I mean, they were just like girls, only... boys. These lines of questioning always made me squirm. Maybe even then, I subconsciously knew I was different.

Years went by like this. Sexual attraction never occupied more than a sliver of my brain space, primarily dominated by kitchen chemistry experiments and the latest scientific breakthroughs.

In fact, the most prominent memory I have of consciously questioning my sexuality happened in ninth grade while I was watching a YouTube video by a channel called SciShow. This particular episode discussed research for a female equivalent of Viagra. In less than five minutes, the show's host, Hank Green, broke down Flibanserin's ability to stimulate sexual arousal in women who feel "little to no sexual desire." This pill was celebrated by many as a way to create gender equality for the almighty orgasm. Women were willingly altering their brain's chemistry to achieve sexual satisfaction, something I had little to no desire for. I couldn't understand why this was such a coveted feeling.

That night, my mind was a beehive, buzzing with unrefined thoughts. Sexual arousal seemed like something I should be aspiring to, but what would it even feel like? If arousal meant excitement, was it essentially the topsy-turvy movements your stomach makes before a big event, but in your vagina? Was that the feeling I had when I really wanted to be friends with that girl in 4th grade? What about that boy in 7th grade? Did I feel the same way about both of them, or were they different feelings?

I lay in bed that night, tossing and turning, unable to sleep and battling to catch my breath. The weight of these questions lay on my chest, holding me hostage, and I realized that I had no answers. I might not be straight, I thought, but I couldn't name the type of non-straight person I was. I worried about the implications of this revelation: Would I be able to relate to friends embarking on sexual and romantic awakenings, which always seemed so intertwined? Would I satisfy my mother's dream of a big Desi wedding or a wedding at all? How would people treat me, and how might my life change?

Although I couldn't wrangle the words to define myself just yet, everything felt on the line.

My high school years were a blur, and I decided against exploring anything sexuality-related until I was in an environment with more autonomy and control. I repressed any thoughts of my sexuality to the deepest parts of my brain, the subconscious within my subconscious. I waited until the right time, which, to me, was college. I would be moving from the Middle East to Canada, and, being away from home, I would be free to detangle the web of questions I had tossed aside.

In my first year of university, I frequently visited many queer *Instagram* pages. These pages welcomed me with messages of hope and affirmation, as well as queer educational resources. The deep dives into sexuality and the wide variety of terminology for various sexual orientations intrigued me. I found myself desperately analyzing all these new terms to find a box that I fit into. During this time, I developed deep relationships with peers from college who were also on their self-discovery journey, interspersing casual conversations with their LGBTQIA+ experiences. The more supportive they seemed, the more I entertained the idea of coming out to them.

Coming out in any capacity is a raw experience, but knowing that the group I was planning on coming out to was so open-minded encouraged my vulnerability. When the day that I decided to come out to them finally came, I remember looking forward to the release, hoping it would be like unhooking a bra at the end of a long day. I anticipated affirmation, hugs, and acceptance.

I was so giddy with excitement that I just let the words pour out of my mouth. I didn't have a clear definition, so I described my desires instead. I wanted to share feelings of happiness and elation with a special someone. My fantasies were of abstract feelings rather than tangible scenarios. I saw silhouettes illuminated by background happiness, but the contents within the outlines remained a secret. I viewed sex as a potential way to get my treasured emotional bliss, a means to an end, rather than the end goal I felt many people viewed it as. I felt pretty indifferent to sex sometimes. All the hypersexualized media made me wonder if I was an anomaly, so I described myself as being within the spectrum of asexuality. I made it clear to my new friends that I was still questioning. I still had a lot to explore, but I was eager to open up about something very personal.

Unfortunately, what ensued was a dismissal, jokes, and flat-out infantilization. I was told that my being unsure and claiming to be on the asexual spectrum resulted from being raised in a conservative environment, referring to my South Asian identity. I was told that I was just naïve and inexperienced, that it was funny and cute that I felt this way.

In all honesty, this mockery hurt more than receiving a typical homophobic response might have. At least, then I could have comprehended the hate as unjustified, and I could eventually work through it as ignorance rather than a personal critique. Receiving this response from people I expected to be accepting threw me for a loop.

I knew I was still questioning; it was true I came from a conservative background, and compared to most of the group, I was inexperienced in sexual and romantic relationships. Maybe they were right?

As South Asian women, we are often taught to be timid and encouraged to stay silent in moments of conflict to save face. We swallow our words and bite our tongues to avoid condemnation and shame on our families. In this situation, standing up for myself felt antithetical to how I was raised to behave. I didn't have the self-assurance to say anything, so I said nothing.

I drew away from those friends and grew protective of my sexuality. I didn't share it easily, and when I did, I found myself being deliberately vague, offering others the opportunity to fill in the blanks for themselves so they might forge an answer more befitting to their expectations. Or, I would go out of my way to justify and over-explain myself, mentioning again and again that I was still exploring. I would say whatever I thought was necessary, trying desperately to show that it was a serious matter to avoid a response similar to the one I had previously received - that my sexuality was laughable.

But how do you prove asexuality when others interpret it as an absence of sex? To me, asexuality speaks to my desire for an intimacy that transcends the need for sex, but in our sex-crazed society, my lack of having sex seems to invalidate my need for more than just sex.

In a world where media representation of queer relationships is hypersexualized, consisting of rushed conversations between two-dimensional characters sprinkled across choreographed sex scenes, I didn't know how to describe a healthy romantic or sexual bond between people of similar genders. I didn't have the exposure or representation I needed to come to terms with this. Even those beloved *Instagram* pages didn't have answers for this deep question: how do I prove my sexuality to the world and myself?

Instead, I was forced to come to terms with my sexuality amidst traumatic coming out experiences and invalidating responses. I felt foolish, and I began believing many of the dismissive comments thrown my way. How could I not be certain of my sexuality at 18+? Was I actually in denial about it, therefore passing it off as questioning? I felt I had to deal with this on my own, terrified of letting the closet doors open to someone new.

So I focused internally first, defining what my sexuality meant to me. I reflected on my first time coming out and why the dismissal hurt so much. I discovered that my desperate search for a term to define my sexuality was more to explain myself to others than it was for my own development. At that moment, I wanted acceptance more than anything else.

Over time, I understood that my sexuality was mine and that I owed no explanations. I also learned just how complex and fluid sexuality could be, and it took me a while to realize that I didn't need to rush in any way, especially in finding a label.

I had to learn the hard way that I am my own advocate. I felt very passionately about my sexuality, and it deserved to be taken seriously. Just as all my feelings and experiences colored my perception of things, other people also have their own palette of colors. If I wanted to get through this struggle of mine, I had to make sure their colors didn't unintentionally bleed into mine. To be at peace with the way I love, I need to be confident in my own canvas, even if it's currently a big, colorful question mark.

I spent a few years reflecting and growing faith in myself. I was finally able to voice my frustration, anger, and hurt to the people I originally came out to. They were apologetic, and I appreciated that, but more than anything, I was proud of myself. My brown girl tendency to hide my opinions and feelings to appease people had been put aside for the first time, and it paid off. Most of them finally realized how hard it was for me and apologized, attempting to understand me better. A few of them still felt the same way they had before. However, I have finally reached a point where I'm okay with that.

Following these confrontations, I gained the confidence to come out to different people in my life. However, this time, I came out to them to practice vulnerability and trust rather than as a plea for their acceptance of my identity. I was able to open the closet door wider each time, and I found my relationships with these people growing stronger.

I came out using the word queer.

The mainstream media depiction of coming out is often a person describing themselves with one simple and definitive label. There isn't a single movie, book, or show I can think of in which someone comes out as 'not straight' or 'not cis;' there's always a specific, palatable label. I choose to use the term queer, an umbrella term rather than a definitive label, which has a special meaning for me: it describes my decision to stop desperately explaining myself. It describes my struggling relationship with my own sexuality. Queer is a beautiful word that states that I love who I love and that I don't fall into the normative standards of sexuality (and/or gender), and that's it. No further explanation is needed.

Those painful days helped me realize that no matter what other people say, I know who I am better than anyone else, and nothing can take that away from me. People tend to act as though their perceptions of others are absolute and accurate, and this elitism is rampant throughout the LGBTQIA+ community. The impact of bigotry towards the queer community from those outside it is well-documented, but the effects of inter-queer bias also need to be addressed. I see this in biphobia, transphobia, and discrimination against non-binary individuals, amongst other forms of gatekeeping in the community. In hindsight, it makes sense that these issues exist within a community that encompasses a wide range of identities. The only similarity is that these identities don't fall into the "norm" of cisgender and heterosexual. But how can we move forward as a community if we don't accept our own first?

Those who cling to concrete labels need to make space for those who dance along the spectrum of sexuality - who dare to explore, shift, or change in whatever way necessary to honor their present truth. Yet, sometimes that truth offers no labels beyond being "non-normative." Although to others, the unsureness of my sexuality might seem like a lack of confidence in myself or denial, in reality, I'm affirming the fluidity of my sexuality. At the end of the day, this is my identity, and I get to decide how to define it, if at all.

Contributor's Bio:

Anna (she/her) is a South Asian woman who wants to share her reflections coming to terms with her identity, the significance of labels, and dealing with unexpected reactions to coming out. She is a graduate student in Chemistry and enjoys mentoring students. She wants to make a positive change in the world and provide support to those who might be struggling with their identity to regain a feeling of control over who they are and how they feel.

Glossary

When Tulips Bloom in Michigan
Malayalam - South Indian language spoken in the state of Kerala

To my Mother, on Queerness, Women of Color, and Revolutionary Love
Kannada - a Dravidian language spoken by the people of Karnataka

The Way I Love
Krishna - Hindu God of compassion, tenderness, and love
Hanuman - Hindu God of strength and energy

All Roads Lead to Slash
Fanfiction - fiction written by the fan of a show (fanfic)
Slash - a type of fanwork in which two (or more) characters of the same sex or gender are placed in a sexual or romantic situation with each other. These works of fan fiction (fanfic) were first circulated in the 1960s through private mail and conventions, and then adapted to available technology - paper zines, members only email lists, FTP archives, eventually ending up on public discussion boards, blogging platforms, and web archives.
Meta - self-referential

Weirdness Points
Kink community - a community of people that enjoy consensual sexual practices that are non-conventional

Not the Beta You Thought You Knew
Kargil war - the war fought in Kargil, Kashmir by India and Pakistan from May to July 1999

Beyond the Binaries
Stud/butch - a term originated from the African American lesbian community meaning dominant or masculine lesbian
Femme - a lesbian that is seen to be more feminine
Stemme - a lesbian that falls between stud/butch and femme
Queer - an umbrella term for gender and sexuality that falls outside of the dominant narrative
Non-binary - someone who identifies outside of the binary of gender (neither woman nor man)
Trans - short for transgender, meaning someone that identifies with a gender that is different than the sex they were assigned at birth
Gender non-conforming - someone whose behavior or gender expression is neither feminine nor masculine
Gender dysphoria - a feeling of discomfort or distress when there is a conflict between one's gender identity and the gender they were assigned at birth
Binder - a constrictive material used to cover one's chest
Top surgery - a reconstructive surgery used to remove or alter one's chest

The Beauty of Brown
Tumblr and gay ships - Social media fandom pairings of mlm (man loving man) or wlw (woman loving woman) characters amongst LGBTQIA+ community members on popular websites such as Tumblr.
Fandoms - communities of fans

Oh, To Be [Perfect]
Ganesha – Hindu God of obstacles
Sanskrit - an ancient Indian language in which old scriptures and epics are written

Editor's Bio

Nithya Elsa Ramesh (she/her/hers) was born in Kochi, Kerala. A beautiful state, dubbed God's own country, in the south of India. At only a few months old, she was wrapped in a blanket and carried onto her first of many flights. Pressure bombarded ears filled her eyes with tears and released inhuman screams from her tiny lungs, a joyful experience for the other passengers, she's sure. She landed in Accra, Ghana, and jumped from her mother's arms into her father's embrace, rubbing against his jagged mustache.

She spent much of her life like this; flying from country to country, city to city, packing and moving, moving and packing. Each stop exposed her to a diversity of culture, history, and people, as well as the injustice that often follows suit. Six years later, she moved to Durban, South Africa, where she spent most of her formative years surrounded by the passionate proclamations of protest as a form of advocacy and reclamation of dignity and respect. Here, she discovered the power of her voice and grew into the activist and the overly opinionated young lady she is today. She also came to terms with her sexuality and grew curious about the different facets of her intersectional identity.

She dove into her passion for social and racial justice while on campus at the University of Michigan. She received the 2020 M.L.K Spirit Award, co-founded a Diversity, Equity, & Inclusion organization, became a trained cross-cultural conflict resolution facilitator, and an intergroup relations facilitator focusing on racial inequity. However, she thirsted for a deeper connection with her Queer South Asian identity and still struggled to find representation and spaces explicitly catered for this intersection.

Before and since coming out at 16 years old, she foraged for the words and representation needed to tactfully explain this identity and its implications to her family and friends, to no avail. Through this book, she pulls together a diverse range of voices that can speak to people across the LGBTQIA+ spectrum and South Asian diaspora in hopes of building the space and community for which she has searched so long.

Acknowledgments

First and foremost, I must thank the 19 beautiful individuals who were willing to join me on this journey. I appreciate how patiently you have collaborated with me, building the plane as we fly, to create this incredible work of art. Your courage, strength, and trust in me made this all possible. We made it through hours of interviews, numerous email exchanges, and multiple submission and editing rounds, and I am so proud.

I also want to acknowledge the community members who were interested in contributing to this anthology. I hope you continue shouting your stories from rooftops, demanding they are heard.

Kori Scott, Mia Heard, and Shartia Ducksworth, the first people I spoke to about this idea. My partners in social change throughout my time in college and beyond. It was an honor to make waves with you three. Your passion, dedication, and persistence inspire me every day, and none of this would be possible without you. Thank you for reviewing these stories multiple times and encouraging me every step of the way.

To Allison Brown, Alina Rosales, Anna Argento, Eboni Sawyer, Halimat Olaniyon, Lauren Nicholson, Manasvini Rao, Sivanthy Vasanthan, and Zoha Bharwani, my editing champions who worked tirelessly to bring this project to life. Your candid feedback, much-needed advice, and months of review helped me realize this dream. I cannot thank you enough for your generosity and insights.

Ananya Mukherjee, thank you for your profound wisdom and guidance throughout this project. You have been incredibly generous with your time and counsel in making this formidable path a little easier to navigate.

To my brilliant artist, payal kumar. Your creativity brought beauty to this project. I walked into our first conversation with no clear vision, and you took my loosely-strung-together adjectives and made something magnificent.

My patient and talented graphic designer, Sofia Zertuche. Thank you for the care with which you handled this project. You transformed words on a page into an immortal text.

Anna Mogill, the first person I trusted to read my contribution to this anthology. Thank you for teaching me the art of vulnerability and self-reflection. Thank you for being my therapist throughout this journey and ensuring I practice self-care while working through these emotionally taxing topics.

Obayda Jondy, my brother and guide. Thank you for always being a shoulder to lean on and going to the ends of the world to help me solve every problem I faced along the way. Your endless support means everything to me.

Susan Wu, my best friend, and personal hype woman. Thank you for your persistent reassurance, for the many evenings we spent crying on the phone together, and for making sure I followed through with this no matter how difficult it became.

To the friends who became family in Accra, Durban, Ann Arbor, and Seattle. Thank you for your unrelenting support and encouragement.

My admiration and gratitude go to the student activists and organizers that challenged me and pushed me to be better in my thinking. I would like to specifically acknowledge Yoni Ki Baat at the University of Michigan, who sparked a fire for storytelling within me, and the Program on Intergroup Relations, who continued to fuel it.

To my father, the first person I came out to. What can I say to my biggest confidant and safe haven? Words don't have the gravity to convey how grateful I am for your open mind and encouragement, even when you may not have known what you were encouraging. So, for now, I will say thank you, I love you, and I will forever strive to make you proud.

To my wonderful mother, thank you for instilling in me the values of faith and hard work. Because of you, I hold God close to my heart, and it was He who guided me through creating this book. Trust in Him and trust in me. I love you.

My grandmothers: Achama, I am strong because I watched your fierce and empathetic service for your community. I am poised in the face of adversity because I learned from your whimsical sense of humor. I would not be half the woman I am without you. Amachi, I think of your ever-smiling face and remember the hardship that hides behind it. I hope, to that length, you can understand how important it was for me to stop hiding.

Thank you to all the supportive friends and strangers who shared their passion for this project, yearning to understand this nuanced perspective or to find their voice amongst these stories. I hope you find refuge amongst these pages.

Thank you to everyone who responded to my cold emails and DMs, even if it was to turn me down kindly. Thank you for writing reviews and sharing this book with your followers. Thank you for showing me how many of us are out there and what we can do when we come together.

Finally, I would be remiss not to acknowledge Rosie Randolph. You deserved more than this world could give you, but your fight and resilience live within me. Remembering you today and every day. This one's for you.